OUR CAPTURED MINDS

OUR CAPTURED MINDS

How religions and ideologies exploit morality to
order and control society

DAVID ANTHONY MATTHEWS

OPRESS

Our Captured Minds

First edition 2016
by OPRESS
PO Box 15221
Vlaeberg
8018
Cape Town
South Africa

ISBN 978-0-620-69344-8 (print)
ISBN 978-0-620-69542-8 (ebook)
ISBN 978-0-620-69543-5 (mobi)

Typeset in 11 pt on 14 pt Minion Pro
Typesetting and design by Trace Digital Services
Cover design by MR Design, Cape Town

To Ewalda

CONTENTS

ACKNOWLEDGEMENTS

I wish to thank Professor Brian Kantor for his continued and enthusiastic encouragement throughout the writing of this book. Any author who has not only a sounding board but a friend of his intellect and generosity of spirit is fortunate indeed.

Deborah Rudman, Martie Oudkerk, and Cynthia Gatter, good friends also, were more than generous with their time and expertise, and I thank them. As I do Thalassa Matthews.

INTRODUCTION

Our personal sense of what is morally right or wrong has a profound effect on our behaviour. What exactly is it, then, that determines the particular moral code to which we each personally subscribe? Why do we each believe what we do morally, what causes us to do so, and why is it important for us to understand just how this comes about?

Morality, the system of values that defines right and wrong behaviour in society, is the single greatest influence on human behaviour that there is, apart from the basic biological drives. Each and every society organises itself on moral principles of one kind or the other. Accordingly, any individual or organisation able to influence what is defined as morally right or wrong in a society is therefore in a strong position to influence what people believe. To influence what people believe is to be able to influence how people behave. And whoever is able to influence human behaviour on a wide scale enjoys a great advantage in the competition of life. The three principal Western religions, for example, owe their success to their early recognition of this fact, and wealth and power have duly flowed to them.

It is therefore no coincidence that the collectively most popular political ideologies in the West, namely, the various forms of Socialism, are also morally based. In the 18th and 19th centuries, following the example of the religions, Communism, Socialism, and Social Democracy presented themselves as morally-driven ideologies. This they did by claiming, as the religions had done, to have identified a great moral wrong in the world. They then, again like the religions, each offered their individual ideological programmes to save the world from this perceived moral error.

The perceived moral wrong in the world selected by the various Socialist ideologies upon which to base their moral crusades was that of the material inequality of men. And at the time there was indeed much that could be considered to be morally wrong in the West with the general dispersion of wealth. Under the monarchical form of government, wealth was generally acquired, not by honest individual ability and effort, but through the accident of birth and patronage, and was thus inaccessible to the vast majority of the populace. In addition, Capitalism, in its early industrial stage particularly, was held to exploit and alienate workers. The very possession of wealth was accordingly seen to be morally questionable by most people.

The moral corollary that the Socialists drew at the time from the gross material inequality, was the demand that all people should be equal, or nearly equal, in terms of their wealth, and the benefits that flow from it. This claim then provided the Socialists with the moral justification that they would need once they were in power, to expropriate wealth from the wealthy, and redistribute it among themselves and their supporters. Even though the forcible taking of wealth by the State from those who possessed it, violated the long-established Western moral principle of the private ownership of property, the taking was held by the Socialists to be morally justified by the unjust and morally questionable manner in which the wealth was considered to have been acquired.

The various socialist ideologies each offered their own particular social and economic programmes for saving the world from the perceived moral error of material inequality, in order to attain a putatively higher moral state of what they described as social justice. These programmes vary from Communism's violent expropriation of all private wealth by the State to today's less aggressive Social Democratic acceptance of a capitalist economy within a welfare state, with the government enforcing the coercive expropriation of wealth from the better-off element, and its redistribution among the less well-off.

What had been true in the 18th and 19th centuries, however, was no longer true by the 20th century. Radical social, political, and economic changes had started to take place in the West from approximately the middle of the 19th century. These were the consequences, among other things, of the ending of autocratic monarchy, the introduction of accountable, democratic government, the extension of the franchise, application of the Rule of Law, improved education, and the remarkable consequential economic growth and spread of wealth that had taken place as a result of these changes.

The majority of people who were now perceived to be wealthy enough to have a portion of their wealth automatically expropriated by the State for redistribution were no longer acquiring it as a result of their ancestry, but actively earning it as employees, or self-employed individuals. And by and large they were earning it justly and honestly, without robbing, exploiting, or alienating anybody else. There was, therefore, no longer any moral justification for automatically considering all wealth to have been illegitimately or unfairly acquired. Nor, most relevantly, was there any longer any moral justification for the State's automatic and coercive expropriation of wealth from the better-off element of society, because the circumstances that had previously been the sole justification for the coercive expropriation no longer existed. The ever-expanding Welfare State, and the politicians party to it, however, had become dependent upon the additional finance extracted from what was effectively the economically most productive portion of the population. These politicians, notably, also included those belonging to the political parties that otherwise declared themselves to be opposed to all forms of Socialism.

The various forms of Socialism did not adjust to the new social and economic circumstances because they were inherently incapable of doing so. As purely reactive organisations, rooted firmly in the negative circumstances of the past, their atavistic doctrines were premised entirely upon the existence of the autocratic and monarchical relationships that no longer prevailed. Their confiscatory economic policy had no relevance in the highly productive modern market economy. So today we find Socialists still making the old, but now irrational, moral claim that a significant difference in wealth among men is not simply regrettable or unfortunate, but is actually morally wrong, *even if the wealth has been honestly and justly earned.* The fact that morality is, *by definition*, concerned only with judging human *behaviour*, and if no wrongful act has been committed by the wealth-earner, logically there cannot be grounds for any moral judgement on the material inequality that their wealth might give rise to, is of necessity, wilfully ignored by all Socialists.

The principal reason that the Socialists today still declare inequality to be an actual moral wrong is because they have no alternative to doing so if they wish to remain politically active. It is the only concept they have in their ideological armoury and they are otherwise ideologically destitute. The implied claim that a moral wrong has been committed serves unconsciously to create the expectation in the public mind that some sort of retribution should follow the implied moral transgression. Accordingly, when the coercive expropriation of private wealth for redistribution takes place, principally via progressive taxation, this is unthinkingly accepted publicly as punishment which is somehow due.

They are assisted by the unthinking and uncritical acceptance of the outdated moral claim by a large section of the public susceptible to Sentimental Socialism, allowing the socialist governments and the politicians of all the other political parties to continue in the lucrative and extortionate practice of expropriating private wealth from the economically productive.

Relevantly, in the past, over a period of two millennia, on the strength of the moral claims that they each made and which their societies duly came to accept, the three Abrahamic religious ideologies gradually took control of their respective geographic areas of the Western world. In the process, they happened also to gain absolute earthly power. Today, while the influence of the religions has declined, that of the socialist ideologies has spread, not only throughout the West, but across almost the entire world. Socialism is the form religion takes in a secular age. They have succeeded in this on the basis of the moral claim that material inequality is morally wrong, and they too have gained temporal power through the coercive expropriation and redistribution of wealth. The mystical and irrational belief that inequality, even that created by honestly gained wealth, is morally wrong is probably as widely and as unthinkingly accepted as self-evident today as was the belief in the Middle Ages that mankind was guilty of original sin, and could only be relieved of it through the agency of the church. And just as the church claimed to represent all that was good, acting on behalf of the poor, the humble, and the dispossessed of the ancient world, putatively out of compassion, even while enriching and empowering itself, so the socialist ideologies today claim the same constituency and motivation as their own. By declaring that their principal objective is to help the underdog, they thereby automatically guarantee themselves the sympathy, if not the support, of every compassionate member of society.

Looking back over thousands of years of recorded history, we thus see the identical pattern repeating itself in all Western societies; the gradual acquisition of temporal power by a dynamic organisation, through its successful manipulation of people's belief systems, always utilising a morally based ideology, which may be either religious or political. We shall be analysing in detail just how and why this happens, and will also show in the process exactly how all ideologies, both religious and secular, use moral and intellectual sleight of hand to create their belief systems and win mass support.

There are two fundamental reasons why both the religious and the political ideologies always use morality as their medium. First, and most importantly, morality is so important to the successful functioning of human society that every society organises itself on moral principles. Human social behaviour being largely regulated by the mechanism of morality, *humans have a strong inbuilt predisposition to obey and respond positively to authoritative moral order.* We instinctively *want* to do what we are told and come to believe to be right. Morality is essentially behaving as other people want us to. This inherent responsiveness to moral appeal greatly simplifies an ideology's task of controlling what people come to believe, so putting the ideology in a position to manipulate their behaviour. *An ideology is no more than a coherent and morally-warranted doctrine claiming to represent the objective truth, that charismatic and dynamic individuals and organisations utilise in order to get other people to do what they wish, through the manipulation of their moral beliefs and desires.* We shall show that not only are religions ideologies, but that the actual content and attraction of seemingly secular political ideologies is spiritual rather than material, and so identical to that of the religions.

While morality is the mechanism by which the individuals in every community relate to one another for their collective benefit, a religion or secular ideology is the mechanism whereby a small group of people control the moral beliefs and the behaviour of the whole community *for their own personal benefit* by playing upon and exploiting the individual's inherent predisposition to respond positively to moral appeal. They both do this by offering an exalted, transcendental worldview. We are all manipulated by one ideology or another. It is by means of ideology that the mass of people in all societies is and has been ordered and controlled by its leadership.

Secondly, morality is by far the most cost-efficient and effective way of controlling and manipulating large numbers of human beings. Physical force, the principal alternative method used historically to control people, is inferior by every measure. A few thousand people may be readily controlled by physical force, but to control hundreds of thousands, or millions of people, as the religions and the Soviet, Chinese, German, and other Western governments have done at one time or the other through their ideologies, a significant degree of complicity on their part is required, *and it is only through morality in some form or other that this degree of compliance can be obtained from them.*

In the course of establishing sufficient moral authority to attract adherents, and then hold them, the various religions created highly convoluted and complex moral dogmas, based upon supernatural beliefs. Morality over the millennia has therefore been the subject of much deliberate mystification and obfuscation by those who have successfully used it to attain their own ends. This makes it difficult for any individual, even today, to get a clear understanding of what morality actually is. This was no doubt deliberate, as was the holding of medieval church services in Latin, a language the peasantry did not understand. Given the dominant role that morality plays in our personal social and political lives, however, it is highly desirable that we each come individually to a clear understanding of it. This is not difficult. In the meanwhile, our minds remain hostage to moral concepts conceived in their own interests by long-dead priests, philosophers, economists, and politicians.

In the process of our enquiry into how morality is used to control and manipulate us through our ideological beliefs, we shall address, among others, the following issues:

- How is morality formed?
- What creates moral authority?
- Where does morality originate?
- Is morality objective or subjective?
- Why is majority-rule undemocratic?
- Why is Relativism so fiercely opposed?
- Is Socialism essentially a secular religion?
- Why do you believe what you do, morally?
- What exactly are Moral Law and Natural Law?
- Exactly what is it that makes theft or lying wrong?
- What morally justifies the coercive redistribution of wealth?
- Are the terms 'Human Rights' and 'Social Justice' meaningful?
- What, if anything, makes material inequality among people morally wrong?

CHAPTER 1

The Nature and Origin of Morality

1.1 Darwin's Gift

Until Darwin presented mankind with a credible alternative explanation for the origin of mankind to that which the church had provided, it was impossible for anyone to contest successfully either the church's mystical explanation of our existence or its claim to moral authority based upon that explanation. If God had created man, and the church was his representative on earth, as it claimed, and which claim was widely held to be feasible, it was fruitless denying that this was true so long as no convincing alternative explanation could be offered in its place. For want of a rational explanation of its origin, therefore, mankind was for millennia intellectually confined to an aprioristic, mystical, and religious world view. This dogmatic perspective altered only from 1859 when Darwin's remarkable insight into the origin of species provided the intellectual foundation for an alternative, non-mystical, and secular world view. ('Secular' is defined as "not connected with religious or spiritual matters".) Darwin's theory has had an enormous impact on biology and science in general, but in respect of morality, Darwin's gift has scarcely been unpacked, and we remain stuck in a largely medieval and supernatural moral mind set, greatly at odds with the technologically advanced world that our rational faculty has fashioned, and in which we find ourselves. (By 'supernatural' is meant, "beyond the laws of nature or the understanding of science".)

The conception of morality that has governed Western human behaviour has invariably been a religious one, based upon belief in God, and thus in the supernatural. It is only very recently in historical terms that a secular conception of morality has been publically considered, and even today, while Western culture is essentially secular, no fully secular and rationally based morality has yet been formulated and put forward. The ethical systems utilised by the West are still strongly influenced by superstition, even though far fewer people today believe that morality is literally God's instruction as to how He wants us to behave. We are living in a period of transition, passing from an age of profound superstition to one where, hopefully, greater reason will prevail. In the meantime, many people are uncertain as to what morality actually is in a secular world – from where its moral authority arises or how its moral laws are formed. Because morality was for so long controlled by the religions, many people have difficulty in believing that morality can even exist in a godless world.

This analysis seeks to clarify the debate around morality, and to outline the basis necessary for a superstition-free and rational secular ethical system. It will also explain exactly how morality is, and has always been, used to control people's minds through either religious or political ideologies, and also the means whereby Socialism, in one form or the other, has come to fill partially the role and the emotional vacuum left by the slow retreat over the centuries of orthodox religion, in the face of the greater understanding of reality facilitated by the scientific method.

While what we have to say applies in varying degree to all ideologies (religions being ideologies), including Liberalism and Conservatism, we focus particularly upon the more aggressive and carnivorous of them, Socialism and Fascism, because of the greater threat that these pose to individual freedom and to a rational and open social order.

1.2 Reason or Revelation

Most people would probably agree that they gain most of the knowledge that they ever acquire throughout the course of their lives through the intellectual process of reasoning. It has long been recognised that, among animals, man has a particularly well-developed capacity for thinking, understanding, and forming judgements in a logical and non-contradictory way. While it is an exaggeration to describe him as being a rational animal, he certainly possesses a strong rational faculty. And it is largely through the process of thinking and forming judgements in a logical and non-contradictory way that we individually make sense of the world we find ourselves in. Without our rational faculty to place it in order, the world around us would probably be an incomprehensible nightmare. Furthermore, as we share the capacity with every other human being, reason provides the logically based and shared understanding that enables us to relate meaningfully and fruitfully, not only to the world around us, but also to one another. It is our common intellectual language. Reason does not by any means give us perfect knowledge or understanding of the reality in which we find ourselves, but it gives us far more than any other conscious method available to us.

3

Many people, however, believe that there is also another way of gaining knowledge that does not utilise reasoning: this is by what is called revelation, the disclosure to someone of previously unknown information by a supernatural source. It is invariably knowledge of a religious nature that is revealed in this manner, often of the existence of a god. Where reason is a product of the intellect, revelation is a product of the emotions.

The principal difference between reason and revelation as a means of acquiring and transmitting knowledge is that the claims to knowledge by reason are required to meet the universally agreed logical standard, while claims to knowledge by revelation are not required to do so. Thus in terms of reason, if somebody claims that water boils at 100 degrees centigrade, they are expected to provide proof of this, if demanded. On the other hand, if somebody claims to know by revelation that the universe was created by a particular deity, they do not expect to have to provide proof of this, because the knowledge was revealed to them personally and so is not directly available to anyone else. It is private, rather than public, knowledge.

While revelation, as a means of acquiring knowledge, cannot be proved either to exist or not to exist, there is no rational reason to assume that it does so, as no generally acceptable proof of its existence has been forthcoming. Until this happens, we all have to rely on reasoning in order to get through life. If one's vehicle breaks down, revelation is not helpful in getting it going again.

What applies to revelation, applies equally to all aspects of the supernatural. We do not know whether or not anything exists outside what we call the laws of nature, or outside the understanding of science. Not knowing, we assume rationally that until it reveals itself to us in some way or other, it does not exist, because there is absolutely nothing that we can usefully do with knowledge that does not exist for us. The majority of people, however, probably still believe that there are supernatural forces and forms of existence outside those that mankind as a whole has become aware of, that affect our lives in significant ways. All belief asserting the existence of God is belief in the supernatural, for example, and the majority of people in the West probably still choose to believe in the existence of some sort of god. They therefore also believe that morality has a supernatural origin, as it is held to derive from him. The supernatural belief that morality is not created by mankind, and that it is somehow objective and universal, transcending humanity, lingers today, even among some who otherwise consider themselves to be firmly non -religious.

As all religious morality is putatively derived from God, it is by the process of revelation that chosen individuals within the various religious organisations that claim to be his representatives on earth come to know what its beliefs and proscriptions are. These favoured individuals then presumably inform their colleagues, who in turn instruct the laity as to what God regards as morally right and wrong. This is obviously a complicated and hazardous process for the transmission of knowledge. Apart from the very few religious leaders who may be regularly in direct contact with God, everybody else has to accept their word that they have indeed experienced a revelation from God and that they have transmitted His word accurately. This requires a high degree of faith in someone who is not known personally to the great majority of believers, and who may well have died some thousand or more years ago. It is, perhaps, pertinent that the word 'credulous' derives from the Latin 'credere' – 'to believe'. So while God's existence is said to be known by revelation, the great majority of believers have in all probability never actually experienced a personal revelation from him. They therefore do not *know* that God exists: they only *believe* that he does, presumably because they have been told so by others, and this is clearly not the same thing. They appear to believe in revelation without actually experiencing it. In this respect, their actual belief in God does not come from revelation at all, but, ironically, from a questionable form of deductive reasoning, such as, "I believe in God because X, whom I trust and respect, believes in Him and assured me that He exists, and that the Holy Book is His Word", or, alternatively, from reasoning in terms of the Argument from Design.

Secularly derived morality, on the other hand, is based principally, if not only, upon reason as it has to align human social behaviour successfully with external realities. (Instinct and tradition presumably also play their role.) Moral beliefs and prescriptions are collectively formulated by communities after rational consideration of all the known and relevant factors impinging upon the behaviour under consideration. Whereas very few people apparently ever experience revelation directly, everybody possesses the capacity to reason, even if this is in varying degree, and so is capable of participating in the ongoing formation of morality. While reason is a vitally important human capacity, man remains overwhelmingly an emotionally driven animal. This fact makes the application of reason all the more important as a counter balance to emotion.

We are not concerned here with the question of the existence or non-existence of a deity, as this is simply a matter of personal belief. We all believe what we want to believe, and we all presumably want to believe what we need to believe. We are, however, concerned here with identifying in rational terms, as far as is possible, the actual origin of morality, as this information will have a major effect on our understanding of it, following the path of reason rather than that of revelation.

1.3 What is Morality?

While there is dispute as to the origin of morality, there is no dispute as to what it is functionally. Despite the control over it that religion has exercised for so long, there is, in fact, nothing at all mystical about it in itself. As social animals, living in groups and communities, the relationships between the individuals constituting those groups and communities are of prime importance if communal living is to be biologically advantageous. This is particularly relevant given the individual's basically ego-driven nature. *Morality, then, is basically the system of values that defines for a community what behaviour by the individual is right and what behaviour is wrong, in the best interests of the community.* It also reconciles the egocentrically driven interests of the individual with the collective interests of the community of which he or she is part. From the secular viewpoint, morality is in all probability a biological adaptation acquired very early in mankind's social development. Morality is embodied in the moral code that, in terms of the secular conception, each com-

7

munity formulates gradually for itself over time, in response to its ambient circumstances.

The system of moral values that evolves in a community does so, no doubt, affected by the actual social relationships of the individual members. It is also likely to evolve in relation to the community's external circumstances, such as food availability, population density, threats to survival, and so on. It should also be borne in mind that we are discussing something that has presumably existed at least as long as has *Homo Sapiens* itself. Science tells us that man is not the only social animal to have its behaviour modified by a moral sense, so the origins of our morality probably predates even our *Homo Sapiens* status.

While the Western religions have had an enormously strong influence on Western morality, claiming it, as God's word, to be supernatural, from the secular perspective sight must not be lost of the fact that morality has all along been solely a creation of the human mind, including even those parts of it that were formulated in the service of religion. In reality, and quite apart from the influence on morality that religion has had, it has always been ordinary human beings in each community who have created and formulated the basic morality governing their behaviour, as an essential part of their social fabric. To this basic morality, the hierarchy controlling each of the dominant religions and other ideologies have added whatever mystical moral injunctions and beliefs suited their interests, and then, generally claiming all morality as their own, declared that there was only one, universal morality and they were the only legitimate interpreters of it.

1.4 The Origin of Morality

Religious Morality

We are here considering two types of Western morality: religious and non-religious, or secular. As we know, the origin of religious morality is held to be God. Knowledge of what constitutes his moral code is said to be transmitted to humans by means of the process of revelation, discussed above, via his professed representatives on earth. In the West, there are three principal religions, each professing to worship the same God, and each claiming, somewhat contradictorily, to be his only, true representative on earth. While their respective moral codes are very similar, having a common origin, they differ in certain important respects. There is therefore not only one religious morality in the West, but at least three similar, but clearly different major ones, each claimed to be the one, true morality by either the Christian, Jewish, or Muslim religion. Within each religion itself there are also sects, which do not always agree with their principal religions in terms of what is held to be morally right or wrong. If one is religious, then, the origin of morality, being God, is held to be supernatural. Exactly what particular moral code one lives by, however, depends on one's particular religion and sect.

While the three principal religions all claim to worship the same Abrahamic God, it is difficult to see how the God who chose the Jews as his favoured people can be the same God who sent his only son to be crucified, and the God who chose Mohammed as his prophet. Certainly, the religious leaders of the three religions each deny strongly that he did *all* of these three things. If he did not do all these three things, however, while each religion insists that he did a different one of the three, logically we cannot be talking about the same God, and therefore the same morality. This is only of interest to us insofar as it reflects on the origin of religious morality, the respective religious moral codes not being by any means identical. All one can say is that there is not one major religious moral code in the West, but at least three, which share similarities and are said to have the same source, but which each appear to be relative more to the different history and culture of the particular society that practises them than to any one, identical God.

Secular Morality
From the secular viewpoint, all morality originates with, and is created solely by, human beings, and consists in those moral opinions that they hold that are not determined by religious or political ideology. There is no rational reason to believe that humans are incapable of creating their own moral codes. If one does not consider it likely that a supernatural being created morality, or that there is anything supernatural about it, then certainly on the balance of probability morality originated with the human species, evolved with it, and is an entirely human creation. After all, where else is it more likely to have come from? There are many factors validating this belief, which we shall consider in due course.

The belief that morality was not created by mankind, but has a non-human essence and origin, is one of the most important and influential concepts in human thought. As we shall duly see, it is the concept upon which all ideologies, religious and secular, rely for their moral authority. It is the glue that holds all human belief systems together.

1.5 How is Morality formed?

We are still far from understanding the process whereby particular types of human behaviour are categorised and transposed by the individuals who constitute a community into morally right or wrong actions. With morality created by the human mind, however, all beliefs that come finally to be categorised as morally right or wrong in a community are, in all probability, formed finally by the consensus of all the community members' opinions. Reason, instinct, tradition, and emotion will no doubt play their parts in the formation of these. To illustrate the possible process: if in a community where incest is practised, it is gradually noticed that the children born to genetically related couples are frequently abnormal in some way or other, and a convincing logical connection between the two factors is made by somebody, in due course it is possible that a majority of the community will come to agree that incest is no longer desirable. At this point, incest will start to be viewed as undesirable behaviour in some quarters, but there will still probably be a section of the community that does not yet agree with the conclusion and continues with the practice which, while being regarded as undesirable, will not yet be declared to be morally wrong. Eventually, when this section of the community is the only one giving birth to abnormal infants, the evidence will probably come to be universally accepted, and incest will then be deemed to be morally wrong in the opinion of the whole community. Whatever the exact process whereby moral judgements are formed, they must logically consist of the opinions of those who form them in the process of responding to the relevant circumstances in which the community finds itself.

11

Morality, then, is essentially human opinion. There is absolutely nothing mystical about its origin or nature. This fact does not reduce its importance or authority in any way, but it is a radically different conception of morality from the supernatural one, with significant and positive implications. As the product of reason rather than superstitious revelation, all and any secular moral claims and beliefs may be questioned and challenged, and must be defended on the grounds of reason. If someone asserts, for example, that incest is morally wrong, they must be able to explain just why it is so. They may not simply say that this is so because they believe that some supernatural source says it is. Secular morality effectively denies any individual or organisation the moral authority to present their ideological moral opinions as actual moral *facts*. All and every moral opinion is understood to be just that, an opinion and not a fact. This denies those who believe that morality has a supernatural source the moral authority that the religions so long abused, to tell others what to believe or how to behave, on the strength of superstitious belief being presented as indisputable fact rather than as contestable human opinion. The current Western moral codes, however, are still far from being completely rational or secular, because of the long, supernatural influence of religion, still evident in them.

While what eventually become universally accepted moral beliefs within a community may originate initially as the opinion of one individual, or of a minority in a community, in order to become fully effective they have to be accepted by everybody, or nearly everybody in the community. Until they are, the behaviour which they govern will not otherwise be sufficiently widespread to benefit the community as a whole, and it is the community as a whole with which morality is always concerned. It is not sufficient for just a majority of people to observe any particular form of behaviour. Everybody, or virtually everybody in a community, has to do so. If they do not do so, it cannot become a communal moral prescription or belief, because not enough people are observing it to make it so. *This practically based requirement for unanimity within a community crops up in many different social contexts, and we will come across it again and again. Unanimity is the basis of moral order.*

Morality is in all probability formed piecemeal over time by the collective opinion of everybody, or nearly everybody (henceforth 'everybody'), in a community. And 'nearly' everybody can be defined as 'excluding so small a percentage that their opinion has no measurable effect'. Once the members of a community reach consensus that a particular behaviour is either right or wrong in a particular circumstance – so far as the wellbeing and interests of the community are concerned – that judgement effectively becomes what may be regarded as Moral Law for that community. Conversely, if everybody does not agree with a particular moral belief, it cannot effectively become Moral Law and remains a minority or sectarian moral opinion within the community.

1.6 The Nature of Morality and Moral Opinion

Being generated and formed entirely by human beings, secular morality (that portion of a moral code that it is not captured or influenced by some ideology or superstition) owes absolutely nothing to the supernatural in any form, either explicitly or implicitly. As previously noted, being based principally upon reason, and consisting solely of human *opinion*, no secular moral beliefs or prescriptions are absolute or incontestable, and no moral opinion can ever be deemed to be a fact. Religiously-based moral opinion, on the other hand, is seen by the religious as being fact inasmuch as it is thought to be expressing God's opinion or will.

If, for example, a religion declares that polygamy is morally wrong, or that killing unbelievers is morally good, then this is seen by believers to be not just somebody's moral opinion, but actual fact. It is therefore much more likely to be acted or insisted upon by believers, than something which is recognised as being no more than mere, arguable human opinion. Religious moral opinion gains a spurious, and potentially dangerous, moral authority because of the belief that, being God's word, it must be true. Some people, human nature being what it is, are, as we know, quite prepared to kill if they believe that the act is in accordance with God's desires and would therefore please him. Justification for such fanaticism is not possible in respect of a purely secular morality, uninfected by superstition, where no moral opinion can be considered to be a fact, and is always recognised as being no more than arguable human opinion.

In the Introduction, the importance to human society of morality was noted, together with the very strong predisposition in all of us to respond to moral order and authority. It is presumably the latter susceptibility which facilitates our relatively uncritical acceptance of frequently absurd and extravagant moral beliefs and mythologies that we would quickly reject as unlikely were they to be presented to us outside a moral context. For example, a widespread belief in the supernatural, or the current uncritical acceptance of inequality as immoral, is no doubt attributable to this susceptibility in us. The most effective way of getting people to believe something that is highly unlikely to be true, it seems, is to present it to them as a moral fact.

While we tend to see morality as being the system of values concerned solely with judging individual human behaviour to be either right or wrong, in terms of the interests of the community as a whole, morality plays a much wider role in human behaviour than we commonly realise. It is a remarkable fact that every ideology, secular or religious, is morally based. Defining an ideology as 'a doctrine giving expression to a set of coherent ideas and beliefs which are claimed to represent objective truth and to be dedicated to attaining what they declare to be the highest moral good', attainment of the perceived highest moral good is, in fact, invariably declared to be the principal objective of every ideology. The socialist ideologies aspire to 'social justice'; Western religion to gratifying God's wishes and attaining life hereafter; (British) Liberalism to the maximum freedom of the individual under the Rule of Law; Conservatism to the preservation of all that is considered best in society and life; and Fascism to the domination of society by an ethnic group claiming racial, cultural, or moral superiority. Morality is the declared objective of every ideology, and so comes to influence our lives in the most pervasive of ways, through the ideology which is predominant in each of our societies.

The psychological or biological predisposition in humans prompting the individual in society to behave in many respects in a way that serves the community's interests before his or her own – the moral instinct – is probably also intuitively appreciated by psychologically astute individuals. This intuitive grasp of the human moral predisposition can present a social danger, however, when it is enjoyed by a Hitler, Lenin, or Mao Zedong.

In essence, morality is the predisposition present in all of us for the individual to accede to what everybody else believes collectively to be the right or wrong way to behave. It functions by predisposing the individual to behave morally as he is directed to do by others acting in concert, rather than acting in gratification of his own immediate personal desires. It is a form of constraint on his individuality, imposed in the collective interest.

This innate moral predisposition renders us all highly susceptible to any psychological manipulation that mimics morality's essential historical content and form. This would be, firstly, if the manipulation claimed to represent objective truth (as religious morality has always done in respect of its moral laws) and, secondly, if it claimed to aim at attaining the highest collective moral good (which is the principal objective of morality). As noted, all ideologies do indeed present themselves in just this form, and they do so because the ideologues who created them were aware, intuitively or otherwise, that by presenting the ideology in a moral form, the chances of it being accepted were greatly enhanced.

Normal secular morality, in contrast to ideologically-driven morality, being free of ideological influence, works organically from the bottom up, each community's

16

moral code being created collectively and consensually over time by the individuals themselves who constitute each community, rather than being imposed from the top down, as is the case with ideologically imposed, command morality, when a community is told in many respects what to believe morally.

In contrast to objective, supernatural morality, truly secular morality:

1. Does not consist of one, universal morality, but many differing codes
2. Is not created by any deity
3. Is created by mankind itself (i.e. is described as subjective)
4. Is subject to possible change over time
5. Is formulated with regard to each community's particular circumstances.

1.7 The Core Moral Code

While all moral codes differ in a number of ways, there are certain moral laws that tend to be identical in every community. These relate to certain actions and circumstances that all humans tend to evaluate in approximately the same way, simply because human nature and needs are similar throughout the world. Murder, theft, lying, cheating, fraud, incest, physical violence, and treachery, for example, are held to be morally wrong, as defined, in virtually every community, just as honesty, self-sacrifice, generosity, kindness, courage, and sympathy are held to be morally good in virtually all. The existence of these similar moral values in all societies is erroneously claimed by the religions as proof that morality is derived from one single, divine source.

Where a society's circumstances and historical experience have differed, however, cultural differences may well be reflected in certain moral judgements and beliefs not connected with the core values. These differences are particularly likely to involve sex, religious observance, and food. The differences in certain moral beliefs of the three Western religions themselves reflect this phenomenon very clearly.

When a religious or secular ideology takes over a local moral system or code and uses it to serve its own interests, the existing code is by and large left in place, and manipulation takes place principally through ideological moral accretion to it. This always starts with the ideology presenting its professed moral opinions to the community as indisputable moral facts – such as that racial interbreeding is wrong, homosexuality is a sin, or that material inequality among people is morally wrong, for example. And it is in accordance with these putative facts that the ideology requires the community to live, once the ideology's moral authority has been accepted as legitimate by the community.

1.8 Moral Authority

Religious
Every moral code requires some sort of moral authority to back it up and to validate it. In respect of religious moral codes, this authority is originally provided by God, and transmitted to mankind by the various religious organisations. Anyone violating God's moral code in the past stood to be severely punished for their transgresson by the religious organisations, and there is no doubt that the fear of violent or intolerable pun-

ishment played a major role in enforcing the religions' moral order. It is a curiosity that while the Western religions were supposedly driven principally by their pursuit of virtue, they should impose it on the populace at times by means of astonishing physical cruelty and violence.

Secular
What provides the moral authority for a secular moral code? The answer is: the moral weight of human opinion, the collective belief of an entire community as to what is right or wrong. Imagine for a moment that you did something in the past that you should never have done, and all your relatives, friends, and acquaintances suddenly learn of your shocking behaviour. They look at you in horror, disbelief, and disgust. It is very likely that you would be filled with a feeling of deep shame, and would wish that you could quietly disappear off the face of the earth. What you would be feeling would be the full weight of communal moral authority, expressed in the emotion of shame. You do not need to burn in eternal hellfire to experience moral authority. Because we are social animals, what others think of us is of utmost importance to us, and any social rejection is felt as a form of intolerable punishment. Social acceptance, or approval, is one of the most important factors in our lives, and something that we generally strive after ceaselessly. And because morality is formed from communal consensus, and we ourselves are normally part of that consensus, to violate it is also to betray in a sense ourselves and everyone who is close to us.

Both Western religions and ideologies feel compelled to derive their moral authority from a supernatural, non--human source. This is unnecessary, as human society is quite capable of generating its own, collective moral authority.

At an individual level, moral authority is the quality that someone possesses that permits them to define for others what is morally right or wrong. (It is not always evident, however, that personal moral authority is derived from personal moral virtue, as it clearly was in the case of Nelson Mandela. Adolf Hitler, for example, also possessed great moral authority in the eyes of many Germans in the 1930s, and yet few people would hold him up as a paragon of moral virtue. Perhaps personal moral authority may be derived also from a charismatic, psychological quality possessed by certain individuals, or, alternatively, the word 'moral' in regard to the term 'personal moral authority' may have a secondary meaning of "related to what is perceived to be the right, in the sense of the *best,* course of action", as opposed to right in the sense of *virtuous.*)

Both an animal's herd instinct and our moral sense express the individual's response to collective decision making within a group of social animals. And once again, we witness the role that the unanimity principle plays in our moral lives. This principle is absolutely fundamental to understanding of human social behaviour.

Sociopaths are a threat to society because they do not share the sense of shame with us. They appear to lack the herd instinct and they know no moral authority.

1.9 The Moral Impulse

Moral authority is the collective moral wisdom of a community. It only comes into existence in the first place because everybody has agreed on the moral beliefs that underlie it. As individuals, we each instinctively recognise the moral authority generated by this fact, and tacitly accept the suzerainty of the collective, and our personal emotional and moral insignificance in the face of it. The moral influence that collective opinion has on us is possibly the greatest and the most enduring and consistent emotional force that we individually ever know in our lives. As the desire to do what we believe other people want us to do, it is perhaps a form of herd instinct, and it is presumably why we have such a strong predisposition to respond to and obey authoritative moral order. This predisposition may be termed the Moral Impulse, and it is the reason why we are all so susceptible to the appeal of ideologies; and also why all ideologies, religious or political, are always morally based, and eagerly offer their adherents a pathway to achieving the highest moral good. (What the ideologues' real goals and motivations are behind the moral goals that they set to attract their adherents is another matter.)

Our need and desire personally to win the approval of those around us, and our fear of their disapproval also goes a long way to explain the human tendency to conform. The non-conformist immediately puts himself in potential conflict with the majority – not a position that the normal person will enjoy or sustain.

The inclination to conformity contributes to the long life generally enjoyed by ideologies, once they have established their belief system over a society.

The moral impulse has a far wider and more profound effect on all our lives than we imagine.

CHAPTER 2

Religious Morality

2.1 The Nature of Religious Morality

In terms of the monotheistic Western religious conception, morality possesses the following five characteristics:

1. There is only one true moral code, because there is only one God
2. God is the origin of all morality
3. Morality is described as objective, meaning that it does not depend on the human mind for its existence (If the human species were totally wiped out, morality would still exist.)
4. It is fixed and unchanging over time, as God has no need to change his mind
5. It is absolute, applying equally to everyone at all times and at all places, and so does not differ relative to the circumstances of different societies.

In terms of its nature, religious morality differs from secular morality in that its primary function is not simply to facilitate action on the part of individuals that is beneficial to a society, and to discourage those actions that harm the collective interests. The pre-existing secular morality attends to this. The objective of religious morality is rather to create the circumstances in a society whereby the populace as a whole is brought to the point where it desires to fulfil the particular and personal objectives of those who control and administer the religion. The religion achieves this by persuading the populace that the religion's moral beliefs and opinions are not mere human opinion, but are divinely created facts. The occult belief that moral opinion can transcend the questionable state of being mere opinion and become actual fact lies, as we shall see, at the heart of all religions and other ideologies.

A truly secular morality, in contrast, free of all superstition and based largely on the one language common to all of mankind, namely reason, would never accept any moral opinion as being fact. All moral opinion would be understood to be just that; nothing more than fallible and arguable human opinion that could well prove in due course to be wrong, regardless of how passionately that opinion was held at any time. While strong moral conviction would be accepted as legitimate, moral certainty would not be recognised, and the truth value of all moral opinion would be seen to be a matter of probability, its accuracy to be assessed ultimately in terms of reason. Nobody would be able to claim that any moral opinion was a fact, on the grounds that it was derived from some deity or other supposedly objective moral source.

2.2 Only one Moral Code and no Moral Relativism

The most important of these five characteristics to grasp is the fact that each of the Western religions, being monotheistic, necessarily claims that there is only one true moral code guiding human behaviour, because they assert that there is only one God and the morality is His, *and that code is the one that only their particular religion preaches.* In other words, each monotheistic religion claims fiercely to have a monopoly on morality and on truth. The supposed monopoly that it has on the moral truth is monotheism's great attraction for the Western religions. It is this that allows each of these religions to claim, contradictorily, that it, and it alone, is the sole source of all truth, and not only moral truth.

Given that each of the three religious moral codes is different in certain important respects to the other two, however, the claim of the three religions to be in sole possession of the moral truth cannot be valid. At best, the claims of two must be invalid, and at the worst, all three are. For each religion to acknowledge that there is more than one true moral code, however, would be to contradict its own claim that there is only one God and only one true moral code, which each of the three claims uniquely to possess. This is the reason behind the Abrahamic religions' passionate opposition to what they refer to as 'Godless' Moral Relativism, which is the belief that on earth there are different, equally valid moral codes, each relative and appropriate to the different circumstances of different communities, and derived from these rather than from a God.

In contrast to monotheistic religious morality, secular morality, were it to exist in pure form, would also posit not just one, but many different and relative moral codes, similar in most respects, because humans are more similar than different, yet different in others.

It is obvious that on earth there are indeed numerous, and different, de facto moral codes in operation, most of which happen to be religiously influenced. To each of the three Western religions, however, the other's codes are not the 'true' moral code. While the three Abrahamic religions all claim to worship the same God, their respective theologies and their holy narratives strongly suggest otherwise. The God who chose the Jews as his own people, and who will in due course send the Messiah to redeem them, cannot logically be the same God who two thousand years ago sent his son to earth to redeem mankind, or the God whose prophet is Mohammed and whose holy book is the Koran.

The three different sets of religious moral law expressed in Canon Law, Sharia, and the Halacha respectively, also differ significantly. Islam even considers Christianity to be polytheistic, rather than monotheistic, because of Catholicism's triune conception of God. The monotheistic Abrahamic religions keep silent on these irreconcilable differences, however, when the issue of relativism comes up, because the one thing that they are logically compelled to agree on is that there is only one God, even though their respective conceptions of that God differ significantly. The empirical existence of actual moral relativism in numerous different communities, however, indicates that the idea of there being only one morality because there is only one God is little more than a necessary monotheistic self-delusion. So when the question of relativism is raised, each Western religion vehemently attacks the idea that there could be more than one 'true' and legitimate moral code, even while they themselves serve as living proof of the fact that there is indeed more than one moral code serving mankind, each being relative to the different cultural and historical circumstances of the society in which it developed.

Curiously, many philosophers who regard themselves as being secular also deny the validity of moral relativism. In doing so, they implicitly posit that morality is not created wholly by humans, and therefore that it is wholly or partly supernatural. We shall be looking at this paradoxical belief in more detail later.

Moral outrages, such as those that take place during times of war, and are still taking place today all over the world, are frequently cited by the religions as the inevitable consequence of moral relativism, when they are, in reality, simply examples of the psychopathic behaviour of which some humans are unfortunately capable from time to time. The religions themselves have been, of course, the very source of much such behaviour.

The religions also at times declare that moral relativists – those who believe that there are many, equally valid moral systems, and not just one objective moral system – reject all morality. They never, however, adduce any evidence for the charge.

All ideologies, monotheistic or secular, must assert, explicitly or implicitly, that there is only one moral code in the universe, to which they have unique access, because they all base their particular claim to moral authority on the assertion that they are interpreting that moral code, and are doing what they are doing in terms of its transcendental moral principles. To acknowledge that there is more than one moral code would be implicitly to renounce the moral authority that the claim to singularity represents. Acknowledging more than one moral code would also imply that morality is in reality a matter of opinion; that it is subjective and not objective. The absolute necessity for the monotheistic religions to deny utterly the legitimacy of relativism may also have contributed to the marked anti-relativist prejudice still evident among many objectivist philosophers today, philosophy and religion having slept entwined in the same bed for so long.

In the pagan, Roman world, there was a multiplicity of different religions existing side by side, largely tolerant of one other. This relatively peaceful, polytheistic order was destroyed, however, with the rise of Christianity and its monotheistic claim that there was but one god, the Christian God, and that all other gods and their moral truths were therefore false. For the dubious theological sophistication conferred by monotheism, religion in the West became rabidly intolerant, and the current crisis of Islamic extremism does not reflect the backwardness of Islam relative to the two other Abrahamic religions so much as the inherently intolerant nature of all monotheism, which legitimises and encourages what Gibbons describes as the strong intoxication of fanaticism.

By declaring that there was only one God, and that he was a morally-driven God, concerned above all with ensuring that mankind strictly observed his moral order, and by further claiming that they were each his sole representatives on earth, the monotheistic, Abrahamic religions put themselves into the highly-advantageous position of being able to decide and declare for each of their respective societies exactly which actions were morally right and which were morally wrong. This ability effectively gave them control of those societies.

In earlier, polytheistic societies, because it was commonly accepted that there was more than one God, each with their own unique, and sometimes conflicting, sphere of authority and influence, there was little reason to believe that there was only one, divinely-derived moral code governing all human behaviour. No individual or organisation was therefore in a position to claim to have a monopoly on the moral truth, as the monotheistic Abrahamic religions were later to do. Under polytheism, any supposedly divinely-inspired moral opinion would be regarded as simply the opinion of one God, or of its adherents, among many, and was therefore not in a position to be claimed as universally incontrovertible truth, governing all human behaviour. The concept of a single and universal moral code, fixed and applicable to all of mankind, on the other hand, flowed directly from the concept of monotheism. Because it was claimed in the West that there was only one God, the creator of all, and a god determined that mankind should obey his very specific moral order, it followed that his was deemed to be the only valid moral code in existence, fixed and applicable to all of mankind.

Given that theistic mankind, whether polytheistic or monotheistic, regarded the Gods as a superior form of existence to itself, and so sought to derive its behavioural norms from them, the transition from a polytheistic conception of divinity to a monotheistic conception proved to be a highly significant one, for four reasons.

First, because monotheism's dogmatic insistence that there was only one God programmed Westerners to accept the corollary that there could therefore be only one moral code in existence, applying equally to all of mankind.

Secondly, it programmed Westerners to accept the idea that their morality was objective, meaning that having being created by God it was not created by mankind itself. This has lead even secular Westerners, while rejecting the idea of a god, to believe subsequently that morality some-

how transcended mankind, originating and existing inde-
pendently outside it.

Thirdly, it programmed Westerners to accept as absolute the moral authority of those who, in their opinion,
command the moral high ground at any time. Initially
this was the hierarchy controlling the dominant monotheistic religions, but subsequently, with the decline in
religious belief, this ready popular acceptance of unitary
moral authority was readily transferred to one or more of
the secular political ideologues.

Fourthly, because the Abrahamic religions each presented their God as offering the individual a pathway
to a superior state of being, provided that they adhered
strictly to His moral law, morality under monotheism
became highly moralistic and prescriptive, as opposed
to the laxer and less morally-orientated behavioural requirements of the earlier polytheistic gods,

The monotheistic religions were thus each able logically to claim a monopoly on determining their respective society's moral truths by presenting what they
declared to be God's moral opinion, not as just arguable
and sectarian opinion, but as divinely constituted *fact*. As
each Western society came to accept the authority of the
dominant monotheistic religion to make its moral judgements for it, revelation was thereby given absolute precedence over reason in regard to all moral issues.

With monotheism, Western society finally turned its
back on Classic and Ionic rationality in the moral sphere,
and adapted itself intellectually and culturally to authoritarian moral dogmatism. This set the stage for the mass
acceptance of the subsequent radical ideologies of Communism, Socialism, and Fascism in the secular twenti-

eth century, by conditioning Westerners over a period of 2000 years to believe that morality was not created by mankind itself, but existed beyond and outside it, and that the moral opinions being expressed by the secular ideologues were therefore not mere arguable human opinion, but true, moral facts created by that undefined force.

2.3 Is Morality fixed or changing?

At the start of this chapter, the fourth characteristic of religious morality is described as being its quality of supposedly being fixed and unchanging over time. This quality arises from the fact that God is supposedly omnipotent and all-knowing. As such, he obviously never has any reason to change his mind. It would be curious, indeed, if an omnipotent and all-knowing Deity were obliged to revise and amend his moral law from time to time. At the very least, it would suggest that He was not quite in control of things. It would also be unsettling if people knew that what was utterly forbidden today might well be approved of tomorrow. The Western religions have accordingly always been insistent that God's moral law, which they interpret for mankind, is fixed and unchanging. That morality is deemed to be fixed and unchanging for all time is a basic corollary of monotheism: if there is only one God, then there can be only one moral code. If any of God's moral injunctions had to change, for any reason, we would not be talking about a morality that forms an integral and fixed part of the universe, but rather an expedient behavioural code that is determined relative to current circumstances; i.e. relativism would exist. This would be anathema to the monotheistic religions.

Although all Western religions and ideologies are based upon the belief that morality is fixed and unchanging, and virtually everybody takes this to be a fact, all empirical evidence illustrates that morality in fact changes over time. Because most core moral injunctions ("do not kill", "do not steal") do not generally change, however, and because change invariably takes place gradually when it does happen, we are not readily conscious of it.

Examples of some of the very many changes in Western moral beliefs that have taken place over time, however, are those relating to slavery, sorcery, judicial torture, corporal punishment, blasphemy, capital punishment, the divine right of kings, theism, minority rule, racism, nudity, animal cruelty, homosexuality, and smoking in public places. Clearly, as mankind's circumstances change, so do any moral beliefs or values significantly affected by those changing circumstances. This allows mankind's moral beliefs to adapt to and align with changing circumstances. A moral code that is not sufficiently flexible to have done this would in the long run have left the code in the Stone Age. The opposition to slavery, for example, took hold only after the Industrial Revolution developed machinery capable of doing society's really heavy lifting, which was previously done by slaves and serfs.

To deny that morality changes over time, and to contend that morality is not contingent on circumstances but is fixed and unchanging for all time, is to claim implicitly, if not expressly, that morality is not created from human opinion, but has another, presumably supernatural, source. The fact that moral belief has frequently changed over time, indicating that it is indeed not fixed and unchanging, would need also to be satisfactorily explained away.

If morality were indeed objective and fixed for all time, we would still today be morally obliged to burn heretics at the stake, stone adulterers and unbelievers, execute criminals, and perhaps even sacrifice virgins. That we are no longer morally required by at least two of the religions to do so, illustrates that they themselves tacitly acknowledge that morality changes, and has done so all along. As an illustration of this acknowledgement, in 1996 the Catholic Church, after centuries of actively taking part in the practice of slavery, came out boldly and declared slavery to be an abomination.

Life for mankind has become increasingly easy over the millennia. In this respect, the life of someone in the 21st century, with an average lifespan of over 70 years, must be radically different to that of an individual 15 000 or even 1 000 years ago, whose life expectancy was less than half the number of years. It is only to be expected, as life has become so much easier, with the change of mankind's circumstances, that its perception of certain things should also change, and its moral judgements with this. In the light of this consideration, it would be very surprising if a Mesopotamian living in 6000 BCE would have shared all the sentiments and moral beliefs regarding animals, the environment, and life in general of a modern Westerner.

2.4 Is Morality Objective or Subjective?

We now come to examine another of the fundamental questions relating to morality, and possibly the most important question of all. Is morality *objective*, meaning in a philosophical context that it exists independently of the human mind, having been created by some non-human, supernatural entity, or is it *subjective*, meaning that it is solely a product of the human mind? Those who are religious say that morality originates supernaturally in God, and is therefore objective, and those who are truly secular say that it is created solely by the human mind and is therefore subjective.

Others who regard themselves as strictly secular, but are questionably so, also hold morality to be objective. We shall be examining this belief shortly. The question whether morality is objective or subjective is undoubtedly the most important question that there is in ethics, and possibly in all of philosophy.

The reason that the belief that morality derives not from mankind itself, but from an outside, transcendental source, morally superior to man, is so important is because this single belief has provided the belief mechanism whereby ideologies, and not only religious ideologies, have been able, and are still able, to gain control over people's minds by claiming to represent and speak on behalf of that spiritually superior source. And by 'people's minds' is meant virtually everybody's mind, including yours and mine.

To answer the question whether morality is objective or subjective: for anyone unwilling to accept the supernatural, morality will be seen to be subjective – solely a product of the human mind. Conversely, anyone believing that morality transcends mankind, and is not solely the product of the human mind, explicitly *or implicitly* believes that it is either partly or wholly generated supernaturally, and is therefore objective.

If someone believes that morality is solely a product of the human mind, logically they must also believe that all morality is simply human opinion. And, as opinion, its truth is always debatable. Conversely, if someone believes morality to be inarguable, objective fact, implicitly they must believe it to have a supernatural origin, because it cannot then be simple human opinion.

Although moral objectivism is the primary characteristic of religious morality, it is also, strangely enough, characteristic of a school of thought that regards itself as strictly secular. Many secular philosophers today tend to be moral objectivists. Even though religion has lost a good deal of its influence on philosophy, it is in the sphere of ethics that its influence is still most evident. All secular moral objectivists deny or question the existence of God or the supernatural, but at the same time, paradoxically imply that morality is nevertheless not simply a product of the human mind; that it possesses also another spiritual, non-human, and exogenous quality. Exactly what this quality is or where it originates they do not, and apparently cannot, say with any certainty. Some think that morality may somehow be a function of the mathematical structure of the universe, or an expression of nature itself. On the point of morality's origin and nature, secular moral objectivists tend to be very vague and ambiguous.

Nor can secular objectivists tell us in what sphere or dimension of human perception morality exists, or how it is revealed to them. They generally hold morality, in transcending mankind, to be part of something 'universal' or 'absolute'. Secular objectivists appear to perceive the absolute, objective morality of which they speak, intuitively, seemingly by some mystical process of psychic osmosis. This would imply that its origin and nature is supernatural. It is seemingly woven into the fabric of the universe, but, consisting of anthropomorphic value judgements as it does, must have been created by some sort of morally conscious entity other than man, because the value judgements embodied in it could not have come into existence on their own.

For a moral system held not to be created solely by mankind, the secular objectivists' beliefs appear to be curiously focussed on *Homo sapiens*. It is never specifically described as the only 'true' morality, because this would too clearly identify it with the religious moral claim to singularity. The secular objectivists' claim that the morality of which they speak is transcendental, however, and so takes precedence over all other claimed moral codes, is tantamount to declaring it to be singular and the only 'true' morality. Its specific beliefs and prescriptions are not, and never have been, identified or written down for perusal and consideration, so there is no evidence that all secular moral objectivists are even talking about the same moral code when they each claim that the morality that they have in mind is objective. Furthermore, it is unlikely that secular moral objectivists from different cultures have the same morality in mind when they claim that it is objective. Like religious believers, when discussing morality, secular moral objectivists tend to avoid the term 'moral code', as this implies that there might be more than one moral system. They prefer to use the unitary words 'morality' or 'ethics', which can be used to imply that there is only one, objective moral code.

To illustrate the quasi-religious nature of secular moral objectivism, consider the disturbing matter of female circumcision, practised in communities totalling more than 100-million people, in Egypt and a few other countries. As much as it appals Europeans and Americans, it is, in fact, held to be morally acceptable by a significant majority of the female as well as the male population in Egypt and elsewhere. The European and American secular moral objectivists would claim that it is unquestionably morally wrong, regardless of what the Egyptians and anyone else believe. This they would hold to be true because female circumcision, in its brutality and assault on the female body, violates an absolute, universal, and objective moral code, held by the secular objectivists to be known *intuitively* by everybody, that must transcend and override the Egyptian's parochial morality.

While reflecting the moral horror that the idea of female circumcision arouses in most Westerners, this secular moral objectivist belief has nevertheless, consciously or unconsciously, to be predicated upon a supernatural belief; namely, that morality is not created solely by humans. This is because, despite the secular moral objectivist's claim to secularity, the origin of any such transcendental moral prescription could only be supernatural, because no purely humanly created moral code can rationally be claimed to be absolute and transcendental, and so to override all other moral codes.

Secular objectivism is, in fact, an oxymoron. If morality is secular, it cannot logically also be objective, because to be objective it has to be created or influenced by a non-human, and so supernatural, entity. In respect of morality, secular moral objectivists believe equally with religious, monotheistic moral objectivists that there is only one, 'true' moral code in the universe. (Invariably, this happens coincidentally always to be the one that they personally subscribe to. Curiously, never in the 5 000-year recorded history of ethics has a philosopher claimed that a moral code *other* than the one that he personally believed in was the true, objective morality.)

This is not to say that female circumcision is not morally wrong, or barbaric. To most Westerners it clearly is. It is only to say that there is no transcendental, universal, or 'true' moral code that makes it so for everybody, and that anyone who asserts that there is, *is wittingly or unwittingly implying the existence of the supernatural.*

It is difficult not to conclude that secular moral objectivists are, in fact, simply closet believers who are too embarrassed to acknowledge openly a belief in any form of the supernatural, but cannot renounce completely a belief that there must somehow be more to life than the empirical evidence indicates, and seek to manifest this belief in the concept of an objective, mystical, and transcendental morality. They cannot bring themselves to believe in God, but they feel compelled to believe in what amounts to a divine moral code. Their source of moral knowledge appears to be a form of intuitive revelation rather than reason. Secular objectivism implies, rather than openly acknowledges, a belief in the supernatural. Despite (or perhaps because of) the ambiguity of their thought, secular moral objectivists have a powerful influence on what passes for secular political thinking among politicians and academics. As we shall see, the mystical belief or hope that there is more to life than our lived, empirical evidence suggests, underlies all ideologies, religious and secular.

The most effective way of controlling the minds of a large number of people, then, is to have them believe that morality is objective and transcends human nature, and that one's organisation represents and gives expression to the transcendental moral objectives putatively embodied in that moral code. Humans, anyway, in general seem to have a strong emotional predisposition to want to believe that morality is objective and universal; hence the irate response from clergy and objectivist philosophers alike to any suggestion that morality is relative. Objectivity, at the very least, suggests that there is a power superior to humanity, and that life therefore has more meaning than we normally experience in our daily lives.

While the various secular ideologies have not each come out with their own, explicit moral codes, simply tacking their particular moral beliefs onto the Abrahamic moral code currently prevalent in their respective communities, implicit in their declared moral beliefs is the objective, and so supernatural, status of morality. They, like the religions, are also moral objectivists, but closet objectivists, as they claim to be secular. By implication, however, they assert that all their moral claims are objectively true, and are therefore not simply a matter of human opinion. This occult and quasi-religious belief is what has justified the killing of Jews and gypsies to Nazis, Capitalists to Communists, and the coercive expropriation of private property to Social Democrats.

2.5 What need do Religions and other Ideologies fill?

Religious and other ideological belief clearly fulfil an important emotional function for most people, if not for everybody, and for this reason alone will always be with us, in some form or other. The underlying emotional need that ideology gratifies is possibly the need, mentioned previously, to believe that there is more meaning, significance, and importance to life than our normal lived, personal experience of it generally suggests. The religious concept of a superior being, concerned with mankind's welfare, clearly fulfils this need for many, and helps them to believe that their lives are not merely the seemingly pointless, lonely, and sometimes frightening existences that they know.

This need for fulfilment is perhaps an aspect of the dissatisfaction quotient that seems to be inherent in us as a species, and that drives us always to want more than we have, and which has presumably led us to dominate the planet. Whatever gives rise to it, this emotional need is possibly the driving force behind the human desire and search for the mystical and transcendental significance that all ideologies, both religious and secular, cater to, and then harness in order to serve their own interests. And is any ideology not simply an idea that holds out the promise of attaining something more in the future than exists in the present?

In our secular age, the Socialist political ideologies have gradually come to occupy the niche created by the slow retreat of revelational religion in the face of the greater rational understanding promoted by science. Religion is a form of ideology that in the West has offered the idea of an omnipotent and perfect extra-terrestrial *being* as the solution to the human need to believe in something transcendent. In the very slightly more sceptical and secular world of today, where the Bronze Age concept of an anthropomorphic deity has become impossible for many people to accept, Socialism is a secularised ideology that offers the idea of a just and perfect *society* attainable right here on earth as its solution to the human need to believe in something transcendent.

The common element in all ideologies, religious or secular, is their advocacy of an idea that appears to transcend, in one form or another, the seeming insufficiencies and smallness of life. The concept of the existence of something, be it an actual deity or an undefined force, morally superior to mankind insofar as it is naturally aware of what is objectively right or best for us, but associated with mankind in one way or the other, appears largely to answer this need.

If this force is naturally always conscious of what is right or best for mankind, vital and profound knowledge that mankind does not generally possess, then clearly it exists at a higher level than mankind. If there is indeed such a thing as a higher level of consciousness or existence, then possibly it is one to which we humans have reason to aspire. This superior existence may be perceived as anthropomorphic, as in theism, or immaterial and undefined, as in deism and the supposedly secular ideologies. Whichever it is, it is always perceived as the source of morality, thereby establishing for the believer that morality is an objective, universal fact, rather than simply a subjective product of the human mind.

For such a believer, to deny that morality is an objective and universal fact is effectively to deny the existence of any force morally superior to mankind. To deny this, in turn, is to deny them the comfort of the belief that life has greater significance and meaning than otherwise appears to them to be the case.

2.6 Religions are Ideologies and Ideologies are religions

While the political ideologies and the religions all utilise morality as the medium to manipulate people and so attain their private ends, they do not, however, share a common moral code. The religions' moral codes are held to have a supernatural origin, insofar as they are all claimed to be derived from a divine, extra-terrestrial source. The moral codes underpinning the political ideologies, on the other hand, are presumably derived solely from the human mind, here on earth, inasmuch as the ideologies claim to be strictly secular. Socialist ethics, for example, rejects the idea of a supernatural or mystical origin for its moral beliefs. Marx said of religion, "It is the opium of the people", and Socialism was deliberately described as "scientific" in order to distance it from any taint of superstition. So while both religious and political ideologies are morally based, the two groups would each deny the legitimacy of the source of the other's moral code. Despite its claims to being secular, however, socialist morality is clearly objective, and so supernatural, as it is held to be objectively true, and not simply arguable human opinion created solely by mankind. Socialists claim that it is a fact that inequality is morally wrong, and not merely their opinion.

Despite the source-related difference between the Western religions and the political ideologies, the religions are nevertheless also ideologies, as previously noted. To explain exactly why this is so, we need first to recall what an ideology is; a doctrine giving expression to a set of coherent ideas and beliefs which, first, *are claimed to represent objective truth* and, secondly, are claimed *to be dedicated to attaining the highest moral good*. The Western religions are no less ideologies in both these fundamental respects than are the political ideologies of Socialism, Liberalism, Fascism, etc.

Most characteristically and most importantly, both political and religious ideologies claim that their ideologies represent the *objective and universal moral truth*. And the fact that the religions claim to be representing the objective moral truth derived from a supernatural deity, whereas the political ideologies do not identify the source of the objective moral systems upon which they base their moral claims, is of far less significance than the critical fact that for both types of ideology the moral truth is supposedly objective (i.e. supernatural rather than man-made*). It is from their common claim to be speaking on behalf of a universal, objective morality that governs all of mankind that the moral authority and power of both secular ideologies and religions arise.* The supposed existence of a deity as the source of their morality in the case of religions is not the most critical factor. It is in people's belief that ideologues, religious or secular, speak as the legitimate representatives of a morality which is not just mere human opinion, but is objective, universal moral law transcending mankind, that their power over men's minds lies.

The fact that the socialist ideologies, on the one hand, deny strongly that they have anything to do with the supernatural, insisting on their secularity, yet on the other hand base all their moral claims on the existence of an objective, supernatural morality, reveals a curious anomaly in their reasoning. The internal contradiction is vivid. This observation applies equally to all supposedly secular moral objectivists.

Religions and ideologies are of course otherwise distinguished by the fact that political ideologies declare themselves to be concerned with the practical distribution of the limited material resources of the earth, while the religious ideologies attend to the spiritual significance of life. They are both Utopian, however, inasmuch as they both claim to be striving for a better state of affairs than now exists in their respective spheres. We all appear to be highly susceptible to the narratives they offer us, given that all societies on earth are organised around one or the other ideology.

The fact that all ideologies, both religious and political, are based upon a superstitious belief regarding the moral authority that they appeal to, either explicitly or implicitly, suggests that mankind is reluctant to accept moral responsibility for itself, and constantly feels compelled to defer to a mystical higher authority. Our ability to reason is apparently ultimately subordinate to our emotional need for spiritual reassurance. And the more passionately a political ideology claims to be aiming at the highest moral good, the more evident its emotional similarity to religion becomes.

To summarise; the theistic religious ideologies gain control over people's minds by presenting themselves to the populace as having been appointed as the agents on earth of a supernatural and extra-terrestrial moral being, which has created mankind and wishes it to behave in accordance with its objective moral code, as interpreted by the respective religions. The political ideologies, in contrast, such as Socialism, Social Democracy, Marxism, Fascism, Anarchism, Conservatism, and Liberalism simply imply that the moral code that they each profess is objectively and universally true, without explaining how this can be so, given that they are supposedly secular. They do this implicitly when each of them infers that their particular beliefs are not mere arguable human opinion, but are objectively true moral facts. That inequality is morally wrong, for example, is an incontestable moral fact for a Socialist or Marxist, and not merely a disputable moral opinion. That the rights of the individual are secondary to the rights of the State is taken as a self-evident moral fact by Fascists, and the diametrically opposed view is held by Liberals and Anarchists.

Once a religious or secular ideology's bona fides have been accepted by the populace, the ideologues are in a position to dictate exactly what in society in their respective spheres is to be regarded as moral behaviour and what as immoral behaviour, because they are held to be the principal or sole source of moral truth. Given the inherent human predisposition to respond to moral authority and order, the ideology is thereafter in a strong position to modify and manipulate collective social behaviour to its own advantage.

As noted, all religions and secular ideologies have the two basic characteristics in common that define them as ideologies. First, they claim to represent an objective, universal (and so either explicitly or implicitly supernatural) truth, and secondly, they claim that their objective is to attain the highest moral good (as defined by them). The invariable presence of these two characteristics in all forms of ideology is highly significant, and raises the question as to exactly what need it is in humans that religions and political ideologies are catering to, that they should constitute the basic characteristics of all secular ideologies as well as of all religions. Their persistent presence suggests that all ideologies are specifically designed to offer something that humans apparently desire strongly, but do not enjoy in the normal course of their lives.

Both religious and secular ideological claims posit the existence of something that transcends earthly human experience. The mere existence of such concepts as an 'objective truth' and the 'highest possible moral good' implies the further existence of a superior level of being, mind, or consciousness than are commonly known. If such elevated things do indeed exist, then there is good reason for people to believe that there must implicitly be more to life than our daily lives suggest, and that this spiritual reality is reflected in the ideology of their choice.

As all human society appears to organise itself in accordance with one ideology or the other, religious or political, this fact suggests that humans are inherently reluctant to accept their seeming existential insignificance and accordingly are emotionally compelled to fashion, not only their religious beliefs, but also the way that they order their political lives so that they present human life as having far greater spiritual significance and importance than seems to be the case empirically.

That it is the primary function of religions to offer a spiritual alternative to the harsh reality of daily life is obvious. What is not so obvious, however, is that the supposedly secular political ideologies are in reality *also specifically designed to cater to exactly the same human emotional need as are religions.* All Western political ideologies, while claiming and appearing to be secular, nevertheless all justify their actions by postulating an ideal, Utopian society representing the highest objective moral good, to be created on earth through the dedicated application of their doctrines. This aspired-to and spiritually conceived society may be either completely egalitarian (Marxist), the epitome of social justice (Socialist), racially pure (Fascist), or the guarantor of maximum personal freedom (Liberal and Democratic), depending on the particular ideology.

The belief system justifying whatever political steps are required in order to bring about this ideal society will also always claim implicitly to represent the objective, universal truth that supposedly governs the universe, thereby morally justifying the (frequently coercive) actions deemed necessary by the ideologues to attain Utopia.

There is little doubt that political ideologies are the form that religion takes for many people in a secular age. Previously, in an age when virtually everybody in the West believed in the biblical conception of God, religion was appropriately defined as the belief in and worship of a superhuman ruling power, and especially a personal god. In a culturally secular era, however, where the concept of an anthropomorphic god is no longer intellectually credible to many people, religion is more usefully understood as the belief in the existence of any form of supernatural existence *morally superior to mankind*. In this sense, ideologies are also religions because of their dogmatic and implicit claim that their moral beliefs are not simply arguable human opinion, but, like the moral beliefs of the religions, objective and supernatural facts transcending mankind.

As noted above, the principal concern of political ideologues is held to be the practical distribution of the limited material resources of the earth. The more astute and perceptive of them are quick, however, to appreciate that their self-interested cause would be greatly assisted were they to claim that their pragmatic objectives were essentially morally motivated rather than materially. This enables them to harness the support not only of those individuals who share their material objectives, but also that of the potentially far greater number of people who share the moral sentiments with which they carefully dress them. The materialistic Marxist desire to get their hands on the wealth (and around the necks) of the ruling classes was thus rather projected publicly as a morally-driven desire for the elimination of material inequality among men. Hitler's political need to create a bogus 'enemy' was advertised as the moral desire to purify the German nation both racially and spiritually by purging it of degenerate foreign elements.

The more radical and extreme political ideologies express themselves via their radical moral objectives, and the milder political ideologies through their more moderate ones. All successful ideologies early realised the great advantage to be gained in attaining their material political objectives by dressing them up and presenting them as a morally-driven cause, so appealing directly to the strong moral impulse inherent in everybody. They set their sails accordingly.

Although it is popularly believed that religions exist to address only the spiritual needs of mankind, and political ideologies exist to do the same for the material needs of their supporters, in practice both equally gain power by making a point of addressing the same spiritual needs of their adherents. While political ideologues have their material objectives, the principal way that they seek to gain the political power required to attain these objectives is by gratifying the all-too-human need for greater meaning and significance to life among the electorate, by offering, like the religions, ideological access to a supposedly higher moral order, validated by what is claimed to be the objective, universal truth. For religions, this higher moral order finds expression in the hope of immortality and unity with God. For the ideology of Socialism, on the other hand, unable credibly to preach so obviously supernatural a doctrine as that preached by the religions, the spiritual needs of the electorate are gratified by the mystical concepts of equality and social justice here on earth, offering spiritual unity with one's fellow man. Religions are ideologies, and ideologies are religions, regardless of the vestments that they are clothed in.

What explanation better accounts for the metaphysical nature of all political ideology, insofar as its *primary* expressed concerns are with a putative objective truth and the spiritual conception of a highest moral good? Listening to the ideologues preach their ideologies, it would seem that the practical and political measures that any political ideology undertakes are there simply to bring about its metaphysical or spiritual objectives. The expropriation of all private means of production demanded by Marxism, for example, is not an economic measure motivated principally by the desire to improve the living standards of the people, but is touted rather as a measure aimed at achieving the spiritual objectives of 'Equality' or 'Social Justice' in the social order. Marx never bothered to provide practical details of the economic system that will supposedly replace Capitalism in due course, because that was not what really concerned him.

Looking back over history, we can readily see the extent to which religion affected and determined the course that people's lives took in the past, religion being the predominant ideology in the West until the 19th century. Virtually everybody's life was influenced to a significant degree by the predominant religious beliefs of their community. This has also been happening, however, to no less an extent in our modern era, driven now by political rather than openly religious ideologies.

Consider the respective effects of the spiritual element driving the ideologies of National Socialism, Communism, Socialism, and even Liberalism on the lives of the various Western populations since 1900. The better to attain their material objectives, political ideologies have clearly also taken over the spiritual role that religion fulfilled for mankind in an earlier and even more credulous age. The more radical that a political ideology is, the greater the spiritual or emotional content of its ideology is likely to be. The possession of a party flag and graphic symbols, in contrast to a national flag or symbols, is an indicator of the degree of ideological radicalisation. The swastika and the hammer and sickle come to mind. Liberalism and Democracy require no flags.

In the light of the above, and defining 'religion' as the belief in any form of supernatural existence morally superior to mankind, it would certainly appear that political ideologies are the form that religion takes in a secular age, with ideologues assuming the function of the priesthood. The personal objective of the ideologues is presumably to attain their own ends, whatever these might be. The method of doing this today, as it always has been for the religions, is for them to provide a credible and transcendental vision which implicitly enhances the meaning and significance of life, for the emotional gratification of their adherents. It seems that human nature is so constituted emotionally that reason will always be dominated by the need for spiritual reassurance, rendering truly secular government highly unlikely.

That mankind, even today, constructs not only its religions, but also its political belief systems, around the belief in a presumptive and supernatural form of moral existence more elevated than mankind itself, is an extraordinary measure of our emotional immaturity.

2.7 The Implication of a Faith-Based Moral System

A faith-based moral system accepts the existence of the supernatural, and allows it an important role in human affairs. A conventionally religious system does so through *explicit* belief in a supernatural deity. A quasi-religious system such as an ideology, or secular objectivist philosophy, does so through *implicit* belief in the non--human nature or origin of morality.

In coming to an understanding of morality, it is important to grasp the fact that *any* belief that morality is not *solely* created by mankind constitutes a belief, either explicit or implicit, in the supernatural. For, as noted previously, if morality is not generated solely by mankind, some or other supernatural force must be playing a role in its generation. For the unconventionally religious objectivists, including Socialists, who or what could possibly create or shape morality other than human beings is generally never mentioned or discussed. The moral system being putatively secular, God, of course, cannot be allowed a role in its creation, and so it is just *implied* that morality somehow transcends mankind – that it exists objectively, beyond us, out there somewhere. It is further implied by Socialists and other political ideologues that, being objective, the moral code on behalf of which they each speak is the unique, true moral code, applicable throughout the universe. And secular objectivists also always mean their own particular moral code, whatever that might be, and not anybody else's, even though there are probably nearly as many different quasi-secular moral codes as there are secular objectivist philosophers.

All moral codes that have existed in all societies prior to the modern era we may assume to have been based upon some belief in the supernatural. As mentioned above in 'Darwin's Gift', there was good reason for this. Since the insight granted us by Darwin's Theory of Natural Selection and by science in general, however, there is absolutely no intellectual or moral justification for us to continue basing our secular moral code upon any supernatural belief whatsoever, which includes any implicit supernatural belief. In fact, it is an alarming indictment of our rationality as long as we continue to do so. And the widely accepted, objective moral beliefs asserted by the socialistic ideologies are clearly still based upon an implicit, if not explicit, belief in the existence of the supernatural. Why, 150 years after Darwin presented his theories to the world, it needs to be asked, are we still using the supernatural to explain or justify anything at all?

The fundamental characteristic of any faith-based moral system is that, believing in the supernatural, it will always claim that morality is objective and universal, and therefore that moral opinion can be a fact. Any society that accepts the validity of this belief, will be governed by superstition rather than reason.

2.8 Socialism as Secular Religion

In his masterpiece, *Capitalism, Socialism, and Democracy,* Joseph Schumpeter perceptively describes how similar the nature is of the beliefs shared by Marxism and the Judeo-Christian religions. This was despite the fact that Marx was scornful of religion, pronouncing it to be the opium of the people. Schumpeter's observation that Marxism was in itself a form of secular religion applies not only to Marxism, but to all forms of Socialism. The shared beliefs of Socialism and religion, as identified by Schumpeter, are:

1. **The existence and knowledge of a system of objective moral values which gives meaning to life and provides absolute standards by which to judge events and actions is believed in and revealed to the believer.**
    (i.e. *For religion* – God's moral order / *For Socialism* – the collectivist and anti-individualist socialist moral philosophy.)

2. The *enemy*, or the cause of what is wrong with the world as it stands, is identified.
   (i.e. *For religion* – The Devil and the human predisposition to sin / *For Socialism* – Capitalism and the Profit Motive.)
3. A course of action is offered that will save and redeem the world from this error and bring it in due course to a state of moral perfection.
   (i.e. *For religion* – Observance of God's laws / *For Socialism* – The Observance of socialist principles.)
4. Paradise is offered (on different sides of the grave, to be sure).
   (i.e. *For religion* – Heaven / *For Socialism* – Social justice and its Utopia.)
5. Those who deny or oppose this revelation are not merely in intellectual error, but in mortal sin.
   (i.e. *For religion* – Sinners and unbelievers / *For Socialism* – Capitalists and all who do not believe in social justice.)

In the light of Schumpeter's observations, it is impossible not to conclude that he is correct, and that Socialism is indeed a form of secularised religion, with an objective morality substituting for a deity. Socialism's self-righteousness, evangelicism, and strong appeal to an objective morality, together with its heavy insistence that there is much morally wrong with the world, classifies it with the religions, and differentiates it in this regard from the other less aggressive, secular ideologies such as Conservatism or Liberalism. The latter are concerned to order society in what they perceive, in terms of their prejudices, to be the most advantageous and morally sound way, but

54

appeal less to the imperatives of an objective morality in order to bring this about. Nor do they justify their desire to order society in their preferred way by claiming, like Marxism, the other forms of Socialism, and in many respects, Fascism, that society suffers a great moral wrong, which calls for coercive correction. Liberalism and Conservatism are more secular in this regard, as opposed to the socialistic ideologies which, in many ways, are more religious than secular in the nature of their idealism.

In rejecting the empirical world in the form that it actually exists, and in claiming to want to change it for something better, both religion and Socialism offer an alternative vision of a transcendental and spiritual state of affairs. They concern themselves less with what actually is than with what, in their respective dogmas, ought to be. In regard to religion, it is God who decides what ought to be. In regard to Socialism, what 'ought to be' is determined by political ideologues and equalitarian academics, speaking on behalf of an unidentified, objective moral code. As the churches purvey abstract, mystical, and transcendental concepts such as the soul and original sin as part of their theologies, so Socialism purveys the mystical concepts of equality and social justice as part of its ideology. It succeeds in appealing to both the conventionally religious and to those agnostics who cannot believe in a deity but who feel the emotional need to believe in something more spiritual than man's secular existence. The agnostics are attracted and reassured by Socialism's solemn (but inaccurate) claims to be strictly secular and scientific. Socialism single-mindedly perpetuates the ancient biblical animus towards, and envy of, the wealthy for its own political purposes. Wealth continues by implication to be morally tainted, even though, as we have observed, there is no longer any justification for this assumption.

While Socialism is ostensibly a secular political movement, it is one that evolved to a degree out of the Judeo-Christian religions. And Socialism, as we noted, like the religions, also operates on the assumption that morality is objective, and is not solely a matter of human opinion. This is illustrated by its claim that inequality is not just unfortunate or regrettable, but is objectively morally wrong. In this fundamental respect, Socialism is clearly not secular, but faith-based. It is the form that theistic religion has taken in today's technological and scientific world, which makes it difficult to believe in the blatantly supernatural. And despite its obsession with wealth, Socialism is not an economic system: it is a superstition-based political ideology presented publically in the emotional format of a secularised religion. Like its Judeo-Christian antecedents, it is apocalyptic and self-righteous, monofideistically claiming that there is only one objective truth, of which it is the unique possessor, and that those who deny this truth are morally defective.

2.9 Why Moral Opinion cannot be Fact

In religious terms, when God declares that one should or should not do something, his injunction is viewed by believers not to be merely God's opinion, but to be a fact. His Word is made fact; it comes to be part of reality, and not merely an opinion, simply by being uttered by God. For example, that God loves mankind is held to be a fact by Christians. Similarly, that it is morally wrong to eat pork is a fact for Jews, and that there is life after death is a fact for Muslims.

In normal and rational understanding, a fact is something that is true, and something is held to be true to all effects and purposes, if it can be shown to correspond with reality. In terms of rational understanding, none of the three beliefs cited above can be described as a fact or as true, because there is no evidence that they do, in fact, correspond with reality. Their truth status, therefore, is no more than that of contestable human opinion. In terms of rational understanding, God would have to be produced as a witness to confirm that the beliefs did correspond with reality. For adherents of the three respective religions, however, they are held to be facts, because they are claimed by believers to correspond with *another* reality that they say has been revealed to them. In terms of secular rational understanding, this argument is not acceptable because what is mutually defined as reality can only be useful if everybody agrees, by and large, as to what reality is, in the first place. And the supernatural, in explicit or implicit form, is definitely not part of the secular concept of reality.

To illustrate the requirement that something must correspond with reality if it is to be held to be true: if I say that I believe it is three o'clock, my meaning is that it is common knowledge in terms of our secular and rational understanding that there exists a system for telling time, and it is now three o'clock according to that system. And if it is indeed three o'clock on several reliable clocks, then my opinion is generally considered to be a fact. (An opinion may, of course, be fallible, if it does not accord with reality.)

Examples of mere moral opinions that have been accepted as actual facts, and so acted upon as such in the West, are that Jews and blacks are subhuman, religious apostates and unbelievers should be killed, and homosexuality and contraception are sins.

Consider how at one time all three Western religions supported the practice of slavery. If in Rome in AD 50, Claudia Voluptua had expressed the moral opinion that slavery was acceptable, she would have been quite correct, in terms of the moral opinion of the age. But in terms of our moral belief today (and that of the Catholic Church since 1996), her opinion approving slavery would have been morally wrong. So her AD 50 moral opinion would not have been a *fact* at the time, even though it accorded with the general moral opinion *and was believed by everybody to be a fact*. Similarly, today's general belief that slavery is morally wrong does not make it a *fact* that slavery is morally wrong. It can at best be only a general *opinion* that slavery is morally wrong.

As with the three openly religious beliefs cited in the first paragraph, above, only if the supernatural being that supposedly creates objective morality were produced could the belief then be said to accord with reality, and so be held to be a fact. People in the West for so long took what was presented as God's word to be fact, however, that many people today who regard themselves as secular still unconsciously accept that moral opinion is, or should or can be, fact, rather than understanding that it cannot ever be more than arguable and personal moral opinion.

The realisation that a moral opinion can never be fact is of inestimable importance in understanding how morality has been, and is being, used to control people's minds through their beliefs. If a moral opinion is held to be fact, then it is not regarded by believers as mere human opinion, but as objective truth. And such truth is revealed to man, not by reason, but by mystical revelation. Consequences flow from facts far more readily than they do from mere arguable opinion. If it is held to be a fact that God hates unbelievers, their killing is far more likely than if no one can say with absolute certainty whether he hates unbelievers or not.

Because moral opinion can never be fact, there is no possibility in genuinely secular morality of moral certainty, or therefore, of the moral fanaticism that it encourages and that it is used to justify. Of course, someone may strongly believe something to be morally right or wrong in secular terms, but they cannot rationally claim as a fact that it is true. Fanaticism is the rotten fruit of moral certainty.

Because moral opinion cannot rationally be fact, what makes murder and stealing morally wrong are not the acts themselves but the fact that everyone agrees that they are morally wrong. The answer to the question whether it is morally right to circumcise all male infants depends on when, where, and of whom the question is asked, rather than on the act of circumcision itself. Many people find this very difficult to accept. All morality is contingent upon circumstances. It arises solely in response to the ambient circumstances in the first place. And circumstances may, and frequently do, change.

Anyone denying the above, and claiming that murder and stealing are wrong, not just because people agree that they are, but because morality is absolute, universal, and objective, would in doing so implicitly be denying at the same time that morality is entirely man made, and would be suggesting that it is, in part or in whole, supernatural.

2.10 How Morality is used to control people's Minds and their Behaviour

The explanation above is important, because the innocent-looking, religiously inspired belief that moral opinion can indeed be fact, and is not mere arguable human opinion, has been the intellectual weapon effectively used throughout history to override man's tenuous rational faculty with superstition, when doing this was to an organisation's benefit. *This is the tool that has been utilised to gain control of society by the individuals and organisations that have controlled every substantial society of which we have historical record, starting before even the Abrahamic religions appeared.* And, extraordinarily, exactly the same manipulative tool is still being used successfully by the various ideologies today, in what is supposed to be an enlightened and secular world.

To illustrate how the process works: to further their particular interests, a group of ambitious, charismatic, and dynamic individuals in a society fabricate an appropriate ideology with a strong moral appeal. In due course they form an organisation, either religious or political, that claims (in the case of religious ideologies) to be the representative on earth of a highly moral, supernatural being, or (in the case of political ideologies) to be the spokesmen for an objective, moral force demanding fulfilment. The moral forces that the respective ideologies claim to represent, will appear to give expression to particular, strong moral opinions, directly concerned with the ideologues' obsessions; such as that God hates unbelievers, or that Blacks are subhuman, or that Capitalism is evil. Having accepted the ideologues' moral authority and the factual truth of their moral opinions, the adherents will then be called upon to rectify the moral error, or failing this, will be required to behave in a certain way, such as kill unbelievers, deny Blacks their civil rights, or expropriate the property of the wealthy.

The transcendental nature of these two types of ideology has a powerful appeal to most people, who, in return for the emotional comfort and gratification that they offer, are more than willing in respect of those matters that the ideologies claim as their own, to suspend the rational understanding with which they otherwise organise their daily lives. They will subscribe to whatever moral belief-system their leaders propound in this regard, as the way to either salvation or spiritual gratification. Believers are thereby able to enjoy the best of both worlds: the irrational spiritual, and the rational material world. Once the manipulators have managed to get the general population to accept that the moral opinions that they declare to be fact are indeed fact, no matter how ludicrous they might be, rationality has been negated and the barbarians are over the wall. Any moral opinion may be claimed as fact. The extent of its acceptance will be in direct proportion to the skill of its propagandists and the credulity of the populace.

The first step to gaining control of a society is to eliminate or minimise the possibility of rationality being used by any of the members of the society as an intellectual defence against the takeover. This is achieved by convincing society that the organisation's self-created moral opinion is not just

61

fallible opinion, but is objective fact. This is only feasible in a society, like much of ours today, sufficiently unsophisticated to believe in revelation as a legitimate source of knowledge. Once an organisation succeeds in having its particular moral opinions accepted by society as being fact, rather than as mere opinion, it is thereafter in a position to define for that society what is true and what is untrue. This is because, once accepted as legitimate by a society, moral opinion is invariably held to be a superior form of knowledge to that gained by reason. The religion or political ideology is then in an unassailable position to declare any possibly conflicting actual facts that may be advanced by any opposition, as being untrue, in terms of its moral opinion.

This is what all theistic religions do when they present what is supposedly god's word as fact. This is what the National Socialists did in Germany when they purveyed the moral myth of racial purity and superiority, presented as spiritual fact. This is what the Communists did when they killed millions in the Soviet Union, in China and in Cambodia on the moral grounds that it was a fact, and not simply an opinion, that all men should be materially equal.

This is what the Social Democrats do today when they claim as fact rather than as opinion that material inequality is morally wrong, and should therefore be eliminated, by coercively expropriating wealth from the economically most productive individuals and redistributing it to themselves and the electorate.

The false belief that moral opinion can be fact is, and always has been, the single greatest threat to individual human freedom, and has been used time and time again to manipulate, control, and effectively subjugate people by leading them to accept as true what is not so.

CHAPTER 3

Facts and Fallacies in the Socialist Belief System

3.1 Principles and Conventions

Before continuing, we need to consider the words 'principles' and 'conventions'. These form part of the intellectual and rational paradigm upon which our civilisation is structured. A principle, the dictionary tells us, is something that is held by a group of people to be a fundamental truth that serves as the foundation for a belief, or system of belief or behaviour. Democracy, for example, is founded upon the principle of the perceived moral equality of all people. This means that if you are a democrat, you accept as a fundamental truth that all people are effectively morally equal.

The fundamental truth that gives rise to a principle is generally one that has been arrived at through experience over time. By observing or experiencing something occurring again and again and witnessing a consistent outcome, a reasonable expectation of the process repeating itself is created. For example, the principle of the moral equality of all people was established in order to protect the mass of people, after it had been observed in the West in the 18th century that throughout history people had previously been regarded as morally unequal, and that this had always lead to the masses being subjugated by one or the other ruling minority that claimed superior moral status. As principles take some time to be established, and generally last a long time if they are sound, abandoning an established principle without very good reason can be counterproductive.

A convention is an agreement within a society on how something should be done, or how it is understood to be. The agreement within a society that individuals possess something abstract that we call Human Rights is an example of a convention, as is the concept of the Rule of Law. Obviously, such things as Human Rights, the Rule of Law, and Democracy do not exist of their own accord in reality. They are called into practical existence, however, when, and only when, people in a community agree unanimously that they should exist and will be held to do so in future, because doing so will be of benefit to the community. The existence of a social contract is another attempted convention, this time accepted by some but rejected by others. A convention acquires full legitimacy within a community only when it is unanimously accepted as self-evidently desirable by all those whom it would affect.

An existing convention may, of course, be challenged, as the Rule of Law or private property rights underpinning Democracy have been in some quarters, on the grounds that they represent the viewpoint, not of all of society, but of the entrenched, conservative element of it. Because these conventions are rationally based, they are always open to challenge on rational grounds. They are not open to challenge on irrational grounds, based on moral opinion being presented as though it were fact, however. The Rule of Law and private property rights may well represent most closely the interests and beliefs of the conservative element in society, but this does not mean that they are not also in the best interests of the whole of society. This is the real issue. The rules of basketball favour the tall over the short, but anybody may play the game and benefit from doing so. At issue also is the question as to whether the opponents of the Rule of Law propose replacing it with another equally rational convention, or whether what they propose to put in its place is based not upon reason but upon somebody's moral opinion being presented as fact. And is what they propose genuinely in everybody's interests, or does it simply replace the sectarian conservative interests with the sectarian and ideological interests of another group? Furthermore, if the Rule of Law is criticised on the grounds that it does not represent equally everybody's interests, then logically what anyone proposes to replace it with must do so fully and meaningfully. Criticism of any long-established social convention is welcome, but any proposals to eliminate or alter existing conventions without a full understanding of their nature and function is very likely to lead to more problems being created than are solved by its elimination.

Democracy was not constructed by accident. It is underpinned by a number of carefully constructed principles and conventions, arrived at by highly intelligent people as the result of a great deal of personal historical experience. All of these are open to criticism, but the removal or diminution of any of them without full awareness of all the implications is very likely to lead to disaster in the form of the Law of Unintended Consequences.

3.2 The Modern Socialist Justification for Wealth Redistribution

The entire socialistic doctrine today, as noted in the introduction, is predicated upon a single moral assertion; that a significant inequality in wealth between people is in itself morally wrong. Everything that all Socialists, Communists, and Social Democrats have ever written or done politically, since the 19th century, has been based upon this one belief. Tens of millions of people have also died, been imprisoned, and tortured under Communist regimes, all because Communists, no differently from the other socialist ideologues, have chosen to declare that inequality among people is morally wrong - and not just morally wrong, but so morally wrong that killing is not an unwarranted response to it. This fact illustrates the power that can be inherent in so abstract a thing as an idea; even so invalid an idea as one declaring that inequality is morally wrong.

It might seem unjust, perhaps, to lump fond and caring Social Democrats and Socialists with hard-line Communists. What does warrant classifying them together, however, is the fact that even though they are by and large fully aware of Communism's murderous record, and no doubt disapprove of it, they do not at all question the basic moral and intellectual assertion regarding inequality that they share with the Communists, and with which they also justify their own political beliefs. It does not seem to concern them that they are politically motivated by the identical belief that consistently motivates the often violent and ruthless behaviour of the Communists.

Before proceeding, a basic feature of current egalitarian theory needs to be borne in mind; it is not simply inequality created by unjustly or dishonestly gained wealth that is held to be morally wrong today, as was the case in the 19th century; it is inequality created by *all* wealth, including that which has been honestly and justly earned. Wealth redistribution today is not, therefore, carried out as a punishment or restitution for the wealthy having done something wrong. Extraordinarily, in terms of modern redistributionist theory, a portion of society is quite arbitrarily made subject to the punitive expropriation of their private property without them having done anything legally or morally wrong.

While inequality produced by dishonestly, unjustly gained wealth can rationally be said to be immoral, because the person who gained it has committed a dishonest act or earned their wealth at somebody else's cost, this imputation certainly does not apply to honestly earned wealth. If wealth has been honestly earned, without prejudicing anybody else, there cannot rationally be any grounds for moral condemnation of the wealth itself, or of any difference in wealth or benefits that it may give rise to. This is even more obvious if the process by which the wealth has been generated has actually been beneficial for society as a whole, which is generally the case today in an open-market, democratic society.

It should be understood that the perceived moral wrong that Socialists use to justify the redistribution of wealth today is not that the wealth was unjustly gained, or that workers are being exploited or alienated – the 19th century justification. Nor is it the existence of poverty in itself. It is rather, simply the existence of significant differences in wealth between individuals, and the benefits that such differences bring about. Expropriation and redistribution today is therefore aimed *principally*, not at eliminating poverty, but at eliminating significant differences in wealth and its benefits. It is egalitarian, and being principally difference-averse rather than poverty-averse, is not inappropriately described as the 'economics of envy'. Redistributionists, like everybody else, of course dislike poverty, but it is not poverty in itself that they actually hold to be immoral. It is the enjoyment by the wealthy of the benefits and advantages that their wealth brings them – and that the less wealthy do not enjoy – that gives rise to the supposed moral wrong of inequality itself. A grasp of the relevance of the socialistic psychological aversion to inequality is necessary to understand the Socialist motivation today behind wealth expropriation.

As mentioned previously, the distribution of wealth in the 18th and 19th centuries under the monarchical political system was reasonably seen to be unjust, and material inequality therefore reasonably held to be immoral. By the middle of the 20th century, however, this was no longer generally true. It might have been true in some individual instances, but no longer applied generally to currently earned or acquired wealth. The question that the practice of coercive expropriation gives rise to today, then, is: on what grounds do Socialists hold a significant difference in wealth to be morally wrong? What exactly is it that they now claim makes it wrong?

3.3 Why Material Inequality in itself cannot be Morally Wrong

Nobody likes or approves of relative poverty, and the existence of an inequality of wealth among men may be considered to be unfortunate and regrettable, but if the wealth giving rise to the inequality has been honestly and justly earned, without prejudice to anyone else, any inequality that it gives rise to *cannot* rationally be morally wrong. The reason for this is that morality is concerned only with right and wrong *human behaviour.* The only thing that morality does, or even can do, is to judge whether a particular action undertaken by someone is either morally right or morally wrong. *It cannot meaningfully be applied to any circumstances that exist or that have arisen independently of anyone doing anything regarding them that is either moral or immoral.* Thus neither bad weather, nor long hair, nor the blue sea can ever be immoral in themselves, because no one ever did anything morally wrong to cause those particular conditions or circumstances.

Inequality created by dishonestly or unjustly gained wealth may logically be characterised as morally wrong, because the person gaining the wealth has done so dishonestly or unjustly. *Neither honestly and justly earned wealth nor any inequality that it might give rise to can, however, be morally wrong in itself, if the wealth-earner has done nothing morally wrong in earning the wealth.* And this remains true even if one takes at face value Marx's long-discredited Labour Theory of Value and his Hegelian concept of worker alienation, which would apply only to those capitalists who employ other people, and therefore do not apply to the vast majority of people today, part of whose income is expropriated for redistribution, who are themselves employees or self-employed entrepreneurs. Of course, as mentioned above, poverty is unfortunate and deeply regrettable, as is the inability of the poor to enjoy the comforts of the rich, but something being unfortunate or regrettable does not make it immoral. When we say that some*thing* is immoral, we are implicitly saying that some*one* has done something immoral to cause that thing or circumstance, because that is what the state of being immoral means. It is meaningless to say that something is immoral if you are not implicitly or explicitly suggesting that someone has *acted* immorally. If any circumstance has come about without anyone doing anything morally wrong to bring it about, then "regrettab*le*" or "unfortunate" are the appropriate adjectives used to describe it, and not "immoral". Such a circumstance has nothing to do with morality.

The claim that any significant difference in wealth, or in the enjoyment of its benefits, is in itself morally wrong where the wealth has been honestly and justly come by is therefore logically unjustified and untenable. No matter how much one might want to believe that it is still justified, it is impossible to do so logically. In the 19th century, when Western society was controlled by monarchies, and before Democracy, the Rule of Law, and the Free Market existed, the coercive expropriation of wealth was morally justified, in terms of today's moral standards. Today, however, because those circumstances that justified it have changed, it is no longer so.

Just think it through for a moment. What could *possibly* make the inequality resulting from the hard work of a perfectly honest person morally *wrong*, in the first place? (And how could the act of the State forcibly expropriating part of the honestly earned income of the better-off portion of society, and redistributing it among other individuals who have done absolutely nothing to earn it, possibly be morally *right*?)

It is extraordinary that the sheer illogicality and irrationality of the claim that material inequality is morally wrong has not been widely recognised and refuted. The belief is as blindly and as unthinkingly accepted today as was the existence of the Devil during the Middle Ages.

The intellectual credibility of the Western religions, sheltered for centuries by the lack of a credible alternative world view to those that they presented to their respective peoples, has suffered greatly from the development of science and from the viable, alternative world view provided by Darwin's Theory of Natural Selection. There is accordingly little place today in the secular world for the host of myths, fables, and fantastical beliefs which the religions have used over the centuries to try to validate their supernatural claims. These, however, have been replaced by the modern, but no less mystical, single concept of the immorality of inequality. Socialistic ideology being a one-legged doctrine, however, with the concept of inequality exposed as false, it collapses, and, with it, Socialism's intellectual credibility.

The concepts of inequality and redistribution were proposed by the socialistic ideologies, supposedly as solutions to the historical problems of poverty and the maldistribution of wealth, which had dogged Western society until the 20th century. The problem of relative poverty is still with us in the West, and has to be addressed, even though it is quite unlike the poverty characterising the 19th century. The exposure of the socialistic concept of inequality as logically invalid does not in any way seek to relieve society of the moral obligation to assist the unfortunate. This was never the intention. No society that regards itself as civilised can fail to provide for the unfortunate. *What this exposure does, however, is to eliminate completely the concept of the moral wrongness of material inequality as a legitimate moral or rational justification for the coercive expropriation of other people's wealth.*

What further suggests that expropriation actually has nothing to do with morality or inequality any longer is the fact that the politicians of all the political parties strongly opposed in principle to Socialism have jumped eagerly onto the bandwagon. None of the liberal or conservative parties are calling for the abolition of expropriation, however, even though it totally violates their basic principles, because the politicians depend upon the money extorted from the economically most productive element in society in order to finance their political activities and the public benefits with which they purchase their electoral support. This tells us a great deal about politicians' principles.

3.4 Wealth Redistribution: Attempting to make a Right from Two Wrongs

The problems that Socialists claim supposedly justify the coercive expropriation of private wealth and income, namely, the existence of relative poverty and social injustice in society, are unfortunate and regrettable, and all right-minded people want them to be addressed on an ongoing basis wherever they exist. This fact does not, however, in any way morally justify Socialism's supposed solution to the problem - the coercive expropriation of private property from people who have committed no crime and who are not themselves the cause of the relative poverty. The coercive taking of private property by the State from any individual who is the lawful owner of it, and who has committed no unlawful act, shamelessly violates the moral standards relating to property ownership long common to Western societies. The private ownership of property in the West is held for very good reason to be a fundamental Human Right. Without it, the individual would not be entitled to even the food needed to stay alive.

In a democracy, the State is entitled to make equitable levies to cover the costs of expenditure incurred for the common good. Income tax levied for this purpose is an example of this, and it is legitimately levied progressively on the "ability to pay" principle, as a concession by the better-off portion of society to the reduced circumstances of the poor. The less well-off are taxed at a lower rate and, below a certain income, are generally excused payment of income tax, while still paying sales tax.

If income tax were levied at only the rate that the poorest could afford, the State's revenue would be so little that a society would be unable to provide itself with anything but the most primitive infrastructure and services. It is therefore in the general interests of the better-off element in society to accept a slightly higher tax rate for themselves, in return for which they, and society as a whole, receive the benefits of the economies of scale achieved by the greater expenditure on necessary infrastructure and services. It is only their voluntary acceptance of this fact which morally legitimises the "ability to pay" principle of taxation, however.

The additional income tax levied on the better-off portion of society for redistribution, as opposed to that levied for common costs, differs significantly in nature, however, in that it is not raised to pay for the collective costs of society. It is levied on one element in society specifically for redistribution to another. It is not so much a tax as a transfer of wealth; an arbitrary and morally questionable taking by the State of the private property of one portion of society and its gifting to another.

While the excusing of lower income earners from the payment of tax at the higher rate is done voluntarily by higher earners, in the common interest, thus justifying the difference morally, the tax on higher earners levied by the State specifically for redistribution is coercive, and the better-off have no choice but to pay the additional tax. There is no moral justification for this.

Socialistic egalitarians argue that redistribution increases what they call social justice in society, and is therefore in the interests of society as a whole. Because it is in the interests of society as a whole, its costs are deemed to be a collective cost, which the better-off should pay because they can best afford it. In the interest of social justice, the egalitarians argue, morality demands that a portion of the property of the better-off citizens should be coercively expropriated from them and redistributed among less well-off citizens, even if the better-off individuals are not in any way responsible for the relative poverty of the less well-off, and the less well-off have done nothing to earn the redistribution. This act is remarkably and paradoxically held to *increase* social justice in society.

This sophistry sets a dangerous precedent for a society that is supposedly democratic. If the State is free to act, not in the interests of all the citizens jointly, but in the interests of one portion *at the cost* of another portion, simply on the putative grounds that doing so is in the interests of society as a whole, so enhancing social justice, then two specific and ominous things have happened. First, the fundamental principle that the State should represent and protect the interests of *all* citizens *equally* has been abandoned. The State effectively in this action has ceased to be the agent for all of society collectively, and serves the particular interests of a portion of it preferentially. Secondly, the principle of equal and just representation has been replaced by a new principle; namely, that the State may act against the interests of any portion of society as long as it can claim that in doing so it is acting in the interest of society as a whole. This new principle, so similar to that under which the Soviet Union operated, is all well and good, if society knows what it is doing in choosing to deviate from the principle of equal and just representation, but there are likely to be certain logical consequences following on from the abandonment of the old, genuinely democratic principle and the adoption of the new, undemocratic one, which society needs to consider carefully.

If the State may act arbitrarily *against the particular interests of one portion* of the people, in the particular interests of another portion, as long as it can claim to be serving the best interests of society as a whole, as it does when it coercively expropriates private wealth, whoever gets to define what "the best interests of society as a whole" are, gets effectively to control the State and everybody else in it. If the State (or whoever controls it) were, for example, to decide, along with the Marxists, that *any* significant material inequality was morally intolerable – and against the interests of society – on what moral or rational grounds could it be resisted? If the State today can legally expropriate and redistribute wealth simply by declaring as its moral opinion that inequality is morally wrong, what is to stop it from executing people, supposedly in order to further increase social justice, were it to claim that executing a particular category of person would achieve this? In terms of Socialist moral theory, apparently any act may be perpetrated by the State, so long as it is justified by the claim that some arbitrary moral good, or greater social justice, will be attained as a result of the act. That the end justifies the means is taken as obvious. This belief has no place in the concept of Democracy, and is a quasi-religious example of somebody's moral opinion being accepted as fact. The Communists in the Soviet Union operated on this basis, and how *in principle* does current Social-Democratic redistributive practice differ?

Once the democratic principle of equitable and equal representation of all social interests by the State is forsaken, and replaced with the arbitrary servicing of sectarian or class interests, Democracy as it has been understood in theory for two hundred years (but never applied in practice) is finished. The democratic State should be, by definition, *everybody* incorporate. To permit it to act in favour of one portion of the citizenry at the cost of another is effectively to revert to the form of authoritarian, minority government that republican Democracy was specifically designed to avoid. Where, how, and by whom are *rational* and democratic moral parameters being set in today's unprincipled socialist dispensation?

That the objective in taking the wealth is presented as attaining greater social justice, can do absolutely nothing to alter the fact that the taking of private property from any individual who is the lawful owner of it and who has committed no unlawful act, is by common moral standards an immoral act. The attempt to rectify the *supposed* moral wrong of inequality by committing the *actual* moral wrong of coercively taking private property from other people, who cannot rationally be held personally responsible for the have-not's circumstances, is no more than an attempt to fashion a moral right out of two moral wrongs.

Just think about it objectively for a moment: an inequality in wealth in society is noted, and judged by some to be immoral. Those in authority decide that to rectify the moral wrong, some of the property and income of some of the citizens who have not committed any crime or done anything wrong must be forcibly taken from them and redistributed among the less well-off. What logical and moral relationship exists between the relative poverty of some and the relative wealth of others that could possibly justify so violent and so arbitrary an action? What sort of morality is it that bleats about the supposed injustice of inequality, and then forcibly and arbitrarily steals from its economically most productive citizens; the very people that society most relies upon for its economic wellbeing? It is highly improbable that morality has much to do with it. The idea of redistribution as the solution to the fictitious moral wrong of inequality is both morally incoherent, contradictory, corrupting, and repugnant. In the name of morality, coercive redistribution deliberately requires the commission of an act of expropriation which blatantly violates common morality, simply in order to realise some illusionary and occult moral benefit. If the private property of individuals who have not been judged to have committed any wrong can be arbitrarily and coercively expropriated by the State, simply in order supposedly to increase some ambiguous moral abstraction called social justice in society, by an unquantifiable amount, clearly society is not being run on rational lines. And, it urgently needs to be asked, what bizarre moral code holds material inequality among men to be a greater moral wrong than the forcible expropriation of innocent people's property by the State? There really is a strong element of irrational infantilism in redistribution as moral theory.

The belief in the moral legitimacy of coercive expropriation is completely irrational and a childish perversion of morality. That one moral wrong cannot be made good through the commission of another has been recognised as self-evident by mankind since time immemorial, for very good reason. It is the first axiom of morality, and coercive expropriation clearly violates it. And the fact that millions of people of good intelligence and good intention in the supposedly secular 21st century unquestioningly accept this absurd moral sophistry as morally legitimate and logically valid raises serious doubts about the rationality of the socialistic social order that has now taken shape in the West.

Concern for the poor is an important social factor, but no amount of such concern can possibly morally justify the coercive expropriation of honestly earned wealth from other individuals as the solution to the problem. The redistribution of wealth, *on a voluntary basis,* of which the 'ability to pay' principle is an example, can benefit society substantially, and can be encouraged in a variety of ways. It accords perfectly with democratic principle. The practice of coercive expropriation for the purpose of redistribution, however, is an entirely different matter, and flatly violates both the democratic principle of equality before the law and the moral principle of private property. And Socialism is, after all, held to be a morally motivated ideology.

There is little doubt that the primary objective behind Socialism's claim that material inequality is morally wrong, is to provide it with a moral justification for the coercive expropriation of wealth from the economically most productive potion of society. The supposed immorality of material inequality is little more than an irrational pretext for the expropriation. We look more closely below at the likely motivation of the ideologues and politicians driving the socialistic doctrines.

3.5 The Real Motive behind Today's Concept of Equality

The original, 19th century reason behind Socialism's desire to expropriate and redistribute wealth, in a grossly unjust and pre-democratic society, was fully understandable from a moral viewpoint. Why, however, are the Socialist politicians still coercively expropriating wealth today, when the social and economic circumstances in democratic societies are completely different, and the original moral justifications for coercive expropriation no longer exist? And why is coercive expropriation still accepted as being morally right by so many decent and intelligent people, the Sentimental Socialists, even though its forcible nature patently violates the fundamental principle forbidding theft inherent in our common moral code?

To answer the first question, as to the politician's real motives, it would perhaps provide perspective firstly to ask the same question in respect of other ideologues who also justified their actions by claiming to be doing good; Socialism's moralistic predecessors, the theistic religions. Looking back over their history, why did (and still do) the respective and successive religious leaders and their organisations claim to be the representatives on earth of a supernatural, extra-terrestrial being who had supposedly created mankind, and who would grant everybody eternal life, provided that they believed in his existence, obeyed his representatives on earth, and did not honour any other gods? Was it because they were so filled with love for everybody else that they were willing to spend their lives, and sometimes even to die in the effort, creating what they knew to be the illusion of an afterlife, simply in order to provide spiritual comfort for others? Or was it because they actually believed that a supernatural, extra-terrestrial being had contacted them and appointed them as his agents on earth? Would it be intolerably cynical to suggest that when they were not actually delusional, on the balance of probability they generally had some other, self-serving agenda, which they hoped to serve by having society believe that they were dedicated to its welfare?

To turn for further enlightenment to the more recent political ideologues who also claimed publically to be aiming to do good: did Lenin, Stalin, Hitler, Mao Ze-dong, Pol Pot, and other radical 20th century ideologues do what they did out of love or concern for the prole-tariat or their countrymen? Were they really striving for greater social justice? Or were they driven by something less altruistic, and far more personal? And do the social-istic politicians and ideologues of today really preach the gospel of equality because of compassion for the poor and a genuine concern for social justice – or are they, on the balance of probability, more likely to be motivated principally by their own, self-serving agendas, imple-menting them by exploiting the sympathy that all nor-mal human beings feel for the poor, and harnessing this and the human predisposition to respond to moral ap-peal, to a highly moralistic ideology, just as the religions have always done? In short, are all the socialist political parties morally driven, existing *primarily* for the purpose of assisting the poor, as they claim, or are they now sim-ply political organisations that are exploiting the issue of poverty to garner public support? The latter motivation would not necessarily mean that all politicians did not personally care at all for the poor. Every decent person is presumably concerned about the poor.

The 19th century social conditions which initially gave rise to the call for the redistribution of wealth in the West have long since disappeared. Where the problem of rela-tive poverty still exists, it is better addressed by economic measures that increase productivity, rather than by expro-priating wealth from the economically productive and re-distributing it. An analysis of redistributive theory makes it very difficult not to conclude that, on the balance of probability, the real objective behind the concept of inequality today is simply to provide a moralistic justification for the political hierarchy in society, working in close conjunction with the rest of what is best described as the predatory elite, to tap into the wealth of the economically most productive element, in order to redirect a significant portion of it towards themselves, thus assisting them in attaining their predatory objectives. Electoral support from the public is obtained by the Socialist politicians with the promise of assisting the poor, and by the offer of a multitude of free benefits for the electorate, paid off, together with the powerful special interests, during the politician's term in office with public money (and public debt).

The predatory elite will consist, as it has always done historically, in those of society's political, religious, commercial, social, military, academic, and intellectual leaders who seek to further their own interests by manipulating the moral beliefs of society, in order to control its behaviour. This is how it has always been. This, among many instances, is how the parasitic aristocracy and church in Europe manipulated and exploited the credulous peasantry for centuries prior to the democratic era. Once again, it is through its moral beliefs that society has always been most readily controlled.

The desire for power and easy money is in all probability the principal motive behind the concept of material equality, as it has no doubt been for all mass movements; helping the poor or eliminating inequality are the pretexts. Despite all its ethical trappings, despite the casuistic moral justification provided by moralising ideologues and intellectuals, the concept of material equality and redistribution is little more than a monumental moral fraud perpetrated upon the economically most productive element in society, and (to answer the second question) complicitly accepted by many of the electorate largely because they misguidedly believe themselves to be its beneficiaries.

Furthermore, given that the concept and practice of wealth redistribution flatly violates the very principle of the equality of all before the law, on which principle Socialism itself is putatively founded, the ideology's claim to be principally motivated by a moral desire for equality cannot be taken seriously. Expropriating some citizens' property and giving it to others, hardly amounts to establishing and protecting any meaningful democratic principle of equality. In fact, it rather violates the equality principle by treating people differently; taking from some and giving to others. Furthermore, the practice of forcing some to work unpaid for others, which is what coercive expropriation and redistribution involves, is characteristic of slavery, not Democracy.

Whoever came up with the assertion that inequality was morally wrong achieved a great propaganda coup, worthy of Joseph Goebbels; they got people to accept as obviously true what was clearly untrue. What had, in fact, been immoral in the 18th and 19th centuries was not material inequality itself, but the *cause* of the inequality in wealth at the time; namely, the social and legal system weighted heavily in favour of the aristocratic ruling class. The inequality was a symptom of the problem, not the cause. To have made logical sense, then, the slogan should have been 'minority rule is immoral' or 'patronage is immoral', rather than "inequality is immoral". The Socialist propagandists were not interested in logic, however, but in manipulating people's minds to their advantage.

Socialism and its heirs, the various forms of Social-Democracy and the 'progressive' political parties, are still-born 19th century ideologies, shunted forward by industrialisation into the present. Their beliefs and attitudes reflect long-superseded conditions and circumstances. Lacking any creative and productive dynamism, reactive rather than proactive, they are negative and backward-looking, and this fact colours both their economic and social policies, which hark backwards to the 19th century rather than working to find viable and fruitful policies for the 21st. Their occult belief in moral objectivism, contradicting their claim to be scientific and secular, is a carry-over from an even earlier historical era. Socialism, in all its forms, is no more than a political ideology dressed up in mystical and quasi-religious garb, presented by the predatory elite in such a way as to provide the masses with a belief system that they see as being dedicated to their welfare, but which is principally designed to keep them quiet, while furthering the interests of the elite.

3.6 Socialism's Deliberate Misinterpretation of the Democratic Concept of the Equality of Man

It is taken to be self-evident today that all people are morally equal. This was not always the case, however, and for by far the greater part of history it was taken to be self-evident that people were morally *unequal*. The concept of equality came to replace that of inequality only towards the end of the 18th century, with the success of the French and American revolutions. And the principle of equality came about specifically as a reaction to that of the historical inequality.

These revolutions were directed against the ruling monarchies, which embodied the ancient and authoritarian concepts of minority rule and the inequality of man. All men being held to be unequal, government was vested in the hands of an aristocratic minority, headed by the king, who often ruled by supposed Divine Right. There were different laws for the different classes, and the law fell harshly upon the lower orders. The aristocracy and the Church were, by and large, also by law exempt from taxation. By today's standards, these conditions were grossly unjust. At the time, however, it should be borne in mind that they were accepted as natural and appropriate by the great majority of people. The democratic revolutions were instigated largely by the increasingly powerful and frustrated middle class, and not by the peasantry, which in France during the revolution often fought on the side of the aristocracy. The near-universal, passive acceptance of the concept of the right of a minority to rule, which characterised Western society right from the beginning of recorded history until the 18th century, is itself a further example of reason being overridden by the human willingness unthinkingly to ignore reason and to accept moral opinion as fact. In regard to minority rule, it was the church's moral opinion that the king had a divine right to rule that was accepted uncritically as a fact by the masses, even though this voluntary subservience was in many respects against their own interests.

The revolutions were undertaken basically as a reaction against the ancient concept of minority rule, by which mankind had always been governed previously. The new concept of Democracy, the rule of all the people, by all the people, was formulated reactively as the logical alternative to minority rule. And the concept of the moral equality of man was formulated as the logical alternative to that of the inherent moral inequality of man. This equality was held to arise naturally from, and to be inherent in, our common humanity.

All men are nevertheless obviously different to one another in respect of their personal characters and qualities, and it is therefore natural that their individual circumstances arising from those characters and qualities should be different. There is absolutely no moral justification in a Democracy, however, for the legal system, in so far as its purpose is held to be the governing of the general relationships of all individuals with one another, to regard or treat any individual, or individuals, differently from the others. In our individuality and the consequences of it we are different, but in the fact of all being rational human beings, we are the same.

This conception found political and practical expression in the principle of equality *before the law,* which is what the masses had purposefully been denied under the old regime. There was never any question of the equality being material equality; equality *of wealth.* The assumption by Socialists today that the form of equality generally articulated during the 18th century democratic revolutions was material equality, is unwarranted, and the deliberate abuse of a concept fundamental to genuine Democracy. The monarchies had only been able to get away with anti-democratic, aristocratic minority rule because people in general had allowed themselves to be persuaded, principally by the church, that the law was an expression of God's will and was different for different classes of people. The principal achievement of democratic thought was to recognise that the only way in future of avoiding the moral legitimisation of minority rule, which was the course that mankind had previously always followed, was if *the law was morally obliged to treat every individual equally, and was forbidden to treat them differently.* Once some men were entitled to be treated differently to all others in terms of the law and legislation, genuine Democracy would cease to exist. Hence the concept of moral equality before the law.

Socialism, in its various forms, has over time effectively hijacked the democratic concept of the equality of man before the law, and twisted it to mean that all men should be *materially* equal. The only way to make them materially equal is, ironically, as has been pointed out by many, by treating them *differently* in terms of the law: for example, by taxing some at a far higher rate than others and redistributing their wealth. *To achieve material equality by redistributing coercively expropriated wealth, it is therefore necessary to violate the democratic principle of legal equality, upon which Democracy itself is based.* To attain its own ends, Socialism has deliberately replaced the principle of the moral Equality of Man with the false principle of the material Equality of Man. As Democracy can only exist in the first place when all people are treated equally before the law, with one or the other form of minority rule replacing it as soon as all people are not, violating the principle has ensured the demise of Democracy as the genuine rule of all by all.

Furthermore, the Socialist's insistence that it was the State's responsibility to engineer this equality turned the State in the 20ᵗʰ century into a major player in society's economic and social organisation. The State replaced the King as the focus of authority in Socialism's political landscape, Socialism proving duly to be every bit as authoritarian as the monarchies had been. This effectively started the process of closing down the highly productive, free-enterprise economy upon the back of which the West had risen to world hegemony, and replacing it with the Socialist Welfare State. Where the average Western State's share of GNP in 1900, during the period of maximum growth and productivity, was approximately 3%, by 2000 it was over 42%, and rising fast.

3.7 The Philosophy behind the Concept of Equality – An Infantile Disorder

The call for equality is more than the expression of the moral desire that people should be equal. It is a call for individuals *to be made* equal, either by revolutionary means or through the coercive agency of the State. Given that no normal person can reasonably be expected to voluntarily give away a significant portion of their personal wealth in order to bring about material equality within their society, anyone who calls for equality to be brought about today, is effectively calling for the State to *forcibly* expropriate a portion of the personal wealth of many of their fellow citizens. No matter how noble their objectives might be, this is what they are doing.

For people to be effectively 'equal', equal can mean only one of two things: that nobody has significantly *less* of certain specified things than everybody else (i.e. a deficiency), or that nobody has significantly *more* of those things than everybody else (i.e. a surfeit).

Desiring equality in order to ensure that nobody should have to go with *less* than everybody else, implies a benign

concern for the welfare of the less well-off, and being altruistically motivated, is to be commended. Desiring equality,
on the other hand, in order to ensure that nobody has significantly *more* than everybody else, is not benign. It cannot
plausibly be motivated by altruism. Such a malign desire is
far more probably motivated by envy or resentment.

Benignly-motivated efforts to reduce inequality will be
characterised by positive efforts to eliminate relative poverty and raise the living standards of the less well-off, by
means which increase their productive capabilities and
skills and by legislation which facilitates the starting and
running of the businesses which will eventually employ
them. Malignly-motivated efforts to reduce inequality,
on the other hand, will be negatively focussed upon di-
minishing the wealth of the better-off portion of society.
This will be done by means of the coercive expropriation
and redistribution of their wealth and the over-regula-
tion of their businesses, both actions supposedly being
undertaken in the public interest.

The inherent contradiction between Socialism's highly
moralistic and altruistically-professed motive for redistribution, and its coercive, immoral methods of achieving equality, exposes the malign nature of its motivation.
It is impossible to take seriously all the pious, socialistic moralising which, on one hand, professes to be pro-
foundly concerned with the well-being of the relatively
poor, and then, on the other hand, proposes to rectify
their relative poverty by forcibly taking wealth from the
relatively non-poor, on the grounds that by doing so
they are doing good in creating equality. One cannot either logically or morally claim to be benignly motivated
bringing about equality when this is achieved by dimin-

ishing the welfare of some for the benefit of others. The two actions just do not rhyme.

The desire for greater equality expressed by the populace at large is no doubt benign, expressing an aversion to the idea of the poor suffering any deficiency. They wish the poor to be assisted (but not, in all probability, if this is to happen at a significant cost to themselves). They are not averse to the assistance of the poor being achieved at significant cost to someone else, however, and least averse if it is at the cost of the well-off. That this involves the theft of private property by the State from individuals who are in no way responsible for the circumstances of the less well-off, does not disturb them because they have been told that inequality is morally wrong and they believe this.

Socialist ideologues exploit the benign (if limited) human predisposition to altruism, and the credulity of the general public, to lead people to believe that their ideological call for equality is, like the public's call, benignly motivated. Their choice of coercive expropriation of private property as the method of achieving equality, however, gives them away and reveals their essentially malign and self-serving motivation.

The redistribution of wealth in the West is no longer seriously justified on the discredited grounds of the Marxist perception of the exploitation and alienation of labour by Capital. Rather than the action of capitalists being the root of the problem, the mere possession of wealth, however acquired, is itself held today to create the perceived moral problem. As we have noted, the entire Left-wing ideology today is built upon the single moral assertion that a significant inequality in wealth between people is not just unfortunate or regrettable, but is actually immoral. The reason that Socialists make their charge against inequality into a moral assertion, as noted in the Introduction, is because the word immoral *implies* that something morally wrong has been done by someone.

Socialism does not justify redistribution openly on the grounds of anyone having committed any moral wrong, but on the grounds of material inequality itself, regardless of how this is brought about. Its justification for redistribution, however, is not made through any open declaration of moral wrongdoing, but rather by innuendo, through the implication that some unspecified moral wrong has been committed which renders inequality morally wrong. While no specific group of people is identified as the wrongdoers, because there is in fact none, this moral implication in turn generates the further implication that if something immoral has been done, the persons responsible for the immoral condition should be punished. The moral wrong of inequality declared by the Socialists to have been committed, has supposedly been brought about by the wealthy, in acquiring their wealth, even if this was done completely honestly. If they had not earned the wealth, the poor would not be at the disadvantage of having less. The wealthy should therefore compensate the poor for the disadvantage that they have exposed them to, by having a portion of their wealth expropriated and redistributed to the poor, so that the poor can enjoy what the wealthy do.

This spectacularly lunatic reasoning, in a nutshell, is how Socialism implicitly justifies what is effectively its theft from the economically most productive element in society. We have seen that Socialists do not, in effect, directly consider material inequality *in itself* to be morally wrong, but rather the circumstance in which the poor are not able to enjoy the benefits and advantages of the wealthy. But they not come out openly and say this – probably because the claim that "it is morally wrong that the poor do not enjoy the same benefits and advantages that the wealthy do" would be unquestioningly rejected by many more people than the claim that "inequality is morally wrong". The concept of inequality would therefore be exposed as simply an opinion, rather than being the moral fact that they present it as. Many people, in fact, would find it quite obvious and reasonable that people who had not earned the wealth that provided the benefits and advantages would have no right to expect them.

With the early Western history of actual economic and legal injustice, "inequality is morally wrong" was a much easier sell. While it is understandable how susceptible the impoverished and poorly educated masses in the 19th century were to Socialist propaganda, the unthinking acceptance of it in today's democratic, affluent, and better-educated society by so many beneficiaries of capitalism's fruitfulness are less easily understood. But perhaps not, if the possibility that many people today regard themselves as beneficiaries of wealth redistribution is taken into account.

We now look further at the concept of equality itself, which underpins Socialism. Firstly, if, as Socialism claims, material inequality is morally wrong, then material equality must be morally right, to make it so. Now, in terms of exactly what moral code is material equality deemed to be, not just desirable, but *morally right?* If it is in terms of a secular moral code, as the Socialists claim it to be, then, by definition, the belief is only opinion and cannot be fact. The concept is not accepted universally in the West either, by any means, so it cannot even be regarded as Moral Law. Logically, the belief in equality is no more than sectarian opinion. As such, it certainly cannot justify rationally the State's theft of private property involved in the redistribution of wealth. Inasmuch as Socialists claim that the immorality of inequality is objective moral fact, and not simply their opinion, the moral code upon which they base their moral beliefs must be a supernatural rather than a secular one. Their belief in material equality is therefore a supernatural belief that an objective morality exists "out there" somewhere, which validates their belief and their coercive actions.

Secondly, the concept of material equality asserts that inequality is wrong because the have-nots lack the benefits and advantages that the haves enjoy. Now, why on earth should it be wrong for one individual to possess something that they have earned through their own honest effort, at nobody else's cost, simply because somebody else does not have that thing? What sort of swivel-eyed moral logic is it that says something can be morally wrong, not because someone performs an immoral act, but because *someone else* does *nothing*? Is an attractive woman's beauty *morally wrong* because less attractive women exist? Socialist moral logic would have it so.

Nothing can be morally wrong unless somebody does something wrong to cause it to be morally wrong, as we have seen. The Socialist accusation of moral wrongdoing where none in fact exists is an example of moral opinion being advanced as fact, and being unthinkingly accepted as such by the public. This blind acceptance encourages Socialists to label as morally wrong all the manifestations of superiority that seem to so upset them, and that drive them to attempt to reduce everything to the lowest qualitative common denominator.

The concept of material equality is manifestly absurd and infantile, seemingly driven by childish envy, and devoid of logic or reason. It appears to be, as Lenin might have described it, "an infantile disorder". People are all too obviously not equal in respect of the various personal qualities common to our species, so where does the supposed virtue of equality originate? What are its intellectual and moral origins? Who says that any sort of equality is desirable in the first place? And why is *material* equality conveniently identified as the type of equality that should be enforced by the State, even though enforcing it violates the very principle upon which any concept of equality itself is logically based, the equality of man before the law?

If, in order to establish what the concept of equality actually means, one attempts to focus upon that element in the concept that identifies just why material equality is held to be *morally* good in the first place, there is none to be found. Its desirability is entirely presumptive. In other words, the moral opinion that material equality is good and inequality bad, is presented (and generally accepted) as fact, without any rational reason or justification being supplied, or to be thought necessary, on the part of its ideological authors as to just why they are so. Apart from the implicit contempt for its credulous adherents that this fact indicates, it also suggests that no rational explanation is given simply because there is none, *and in terms of revelational practice,* none is to be expected.

Moving forward past this lacuna, and examining the moral landscape, it becomes difficult not to conclude that the only reason that Socialist ideologues declared material inequality to be morally wrong was because it was by far the easiest way for them to win electoral support, and so power. The poor, who gradually came to constitute the electoral majority as the vote was extended throughout the 19th and 20th centuries, naturally wanted to enjoy the benefits and advantages that the wealthy did, but had little chance of doing so in the social and economic dispensation of the earlier centuries. Nobody was aware of the enormous social upliftment that the increasingly liberalised government and market was to bring about in the West over the last decades of the 19th and all of the 20th century. The socialistic, dog-in-the-manger doctrine of expropriating and redistributing wealth, which was to prove so counter-productive in the 21st century because of its corrupting influence on society, appeared at the time to be an easy, attractive and viable economic proposition. Because in terms of general Western morality, theft was clearly wrong, however, the redistributive theft from the better-off element that was to take place had to be legitimised. Accordingly, the Socialist ideologues formulated the supposedly moral concept of material inequality to justify it. Unable to justify their own theft from the economically most productive element in society by describing it as being punishment for dishonesty, they instead levelled the charge of immorality, not against any specific guilty *person or persons,* which logic required, but against the *condition* of inequality of wealth itself. This is the moral and intellectual sleight-of-hand mentioned in the introduction, which has been complicitly overlooked by the faithful ever since.

Although the concept of equality has been uncritically accepted as legitimate by nearly everybody, it nevertheless should, given the major role it plays in society today, but above all, simply in the name of reason, automatically give rise to numerous questions. For example, does the principle of equality require *absolute* material equality among men, or not? And, if not, why not? At what degree of difference in wealth is the state of moral wrongness attained, if absolute equality is not required? And what brings it into being at that point? Is it perhaps the sudden appearance of a feeling of discontent in those who have less? If not, exactly what phenomenon is it that creates the moral wrong? And who says that it does so at that particular point, and what are their qualifications for making such a judgement? If material equality were ever to be attained, would the State thereafter enforce equality on an ongoing basis, by preventing individuals by law from doing anything that would enable them to earn more than the majority, and thereby reintroduce inequality? And if not, why not, because within a few years the industrious and talented few would have earned and saved more than the majority, thus creating inequality once again? Would this recrudescence of inequality be tolerable? And so on, and on, and on. Why is the obviously puerile and incoherent moralising characteristic of Socialism so unquestioningly and docilely accepted as legitimate by so many people?

The socialist belief that the supposed moral wrong of material inequality among men can only be made good by coercively expropriating the wealth of people who have done no wrong, is cut from the same threadbare cloth as the mystical, medieval belief that man was born sinful, and could only gain redemption by confessing his sins and paying penance. Each belief is characterised by the irrational moral assumption that something that does not exist in reality, does exist, and is of utmost moral importance. As the medieval church's belief system was constructed upon outlandish moral assumptions and fantasies, so the entire, infantile, socialist ideology today is constructed upon its single, mystical moral assertion. The excuse that the socialist ideologies have found for their extortionate policies – the irrational claim that inequality is morally wrong – is so nonsensical and inane in today's circumstances, that its success in being so widely accepted today as logically valid and morally legitimate raises serious questions about our persistent and seemingly limitless human credulity, not to say intelligence, in what we hold to be a sophisticated and secular age.

3.8 The Socialist Abuse of the Concept of Human Rights

In the light of mankind's negative historical experience with aristocratic minority rule, the 18th century French and American democratic revolutionaries identified the political concept that they believed would best protect the masses from exploitation by the strong. As it had been the long, historical acceptance by everybody of the principle of minority rule that had resulted in the majority being exploited by one or the other minority throughout the course of history, the Democrats established the principle of the moral equality of all men in reaction to that of minority rule. Henceforth, no individual, or group of individuals, would be recognised as having the inherent moral right to rule over anyone else. And as it had been by means of the application of different legal principles and laws for the various social classes that the aristocracy had maintained their dominance over the general population, the Democrats anchored the concept of man's moral equality in the concept of the equality of all men before the law. The concept of the equality of all men was fundamentally reactive and defensive, to protect them from one another, and from minority authoritarianism.

To further protect the concept of moral equality, the Democrats identified what they believed should be regarded as fundamental human political rights, arising also from our common humanity, and which they saw as being inherent in the democratic conception of society. These were held to be absolutely essential in protecting the citizens' freedom from the type of excessive political authority that they had so recently experienced at the hands of the monarchy. These rights, which are referred to as *First Generation Rights,* consist, besides that to equality before the law, to the right to life and liberty; to free speech; to freedom of movement and assembly; to religious freedom; to a free press; to regular free and fair elections, and to the private ownership of property. They are expressed in the 18th century French Bill of Human Rights and elsewhere, and are held to take precedence over any other rights, *insofar as no other human rights are likely to exist for long if these fundamental rights are not faithfully observed at all times.*

Three important characteristic features of these fundamental rights identify them as legitimate democratic human rights. These are, firstly, that they are rights that everyone would want *themselves* to possess, because of the political protection that they provide the individual, against excessive State authority. Secondly, and most importantly, that they are rights that nobody, in terms of democratic principles, can legitimately deny to *anyone else*. Thirdly, that they are cost-free, in the sense that nobody else is required to pay for them, or is put at any disadvantage by them, and therefore they are acceptable to everybody. In all three respects, they comply with the unanimity principle.

Shortly after the Second World War, additional Human Rights, known today as the Second-Generation Rights, were proposed by the Left and, after being incorporated in the United Nations Bill of Human Rights, have come to be widely accepted as legitimate. These rights are essentially economic entitlements, rather than rights, and include the entitlements to health-care, education, housing, employment, and social-security. Subsequently, a Third Generation of social rights has been proposed. This includes, among other things, the entitlements to a healthy environment, to social development, and to something described as intergenerational equity.

What are referred to as the Second and Third Generation Rights differ radically from the original political First Generation Rights in two respects. First, unlike the First Generation Rights, they are not cost-free. There is always a financial cost attached to their implementation which *someone other than the beneficiaries is expected to pay.* They are therefore radically different in nature from the original rights, where there was no question of any individual having to provide the wherewithal for the Human Rights of any other person. They have clearly been evoked to provide a further justification for redistributing wealth. Human Rights cannot meaningfully be self-granted, or granted willy-nilly by some authority to its supporters. To be meaningful, Human Rights have, by definition, to arise from our common humanity, and have to be so self-evidently desirable that they are unquestioningly agreed to by everybody. i.e. the unanimity principle must apply. They cannot rationally be entitlements granted to some at the cost of others.

If something is to be claimed legitimately to arise from our common humanity, it must be common to each and every individual, by definition, and without exception. Housing, food, clothing, education, health-care, and employment are certainly required by every individual, but these are human *needs*. Needs should not be confused with rights. Just because everyone needs certain things does not mean that they are automatically entitled to them. And a supposed right that has to be paid for by someone else, cannot coherently be claimed to arise from our common humanity.

Secondly, Second and Third Generation Rights do not comply with the unanimity principle: they are not accepted as legitimate democratic Human Rights by everybody. On the contrary, they are strongly, and understandably, opposed by those who have to pay the cost of them. They cannot, therefore, rationally be said to arise naturally from either our common humanity or from democratic principle.

This is not to say that everybody in society should not enjoy the Second Generation Rights if a society can afford them, and if everybody is willing to contribute their fair share to the cost of providing them. It is simply to say that to be classified rationally and meaningfully as a genuine Human Right, the supposed Right has to comply with certain logical and rational requirements.

The original democratic concept of Human Rights was legitimised by the general understanding and acceptance that the defined Human Rights were to be regarded as inherent in our common humanity and arose from it. This being perceived to be a universal truth, the concept was elevated to the status of principle. The Second and Third Generation rights, in view of the two defects mentioned above, do not qualify in any meaningful way as Human Rights. That they have been claimed as such is characteristic of the intellectual and moral sleight of hand that Socialism utilises in order to attain its ends. Once again, we see how morality is used to control people's minds by presenting what is no more than personal moral opinion as indisputable moral fact.

3.9 The Counterfeit Term 'Social Justice'

The term 'social justice' is a favourite among Socialists, used as though it were heavy with import. In reality, the term adds nothing in meaning to the ancient, single word 'justice'. In standard English, the word 'justice' means "the quality of being equally fair and reasonable to everybody". 'Social' means "relating to society". The two words joined therefore mean, "the quality of being equally fair and reasonable to everybody in society". The word 'Social' ("relating to society") is tautological as it means no more than the words "to everybody". It adds nothing to the broader meaning of the word 'justice'. The term 'Social Justice', *as it stands,* therefore means no more than the word 'justice' does alone. It is fatuous and superfluous, and the question arises as to why the term was coined.

The answer, in all probability, is because the term is intended to be a euphemism. When Socialists call for social justice, they are not using the two joined words with their standard meaning, because, as we have noted, this is no more than the word 'justice' alone. What they actually mean is, "the circumstance wherein everybody is entitled to share equally in the dispersion of the wealth that society produces". This is a euphemism for the redistribution of wealth. Rather than coming out honestly and calling directly for the redistribution of wealth, and so alarming the horses, Socialists prefer to disguise their real objectives, and to clothe them in Orwellian Newspeak. Test this for yourself next time that you come across the term 'social justice': replace it firstly with "what is equally fair and reasonable to everybody", and then with "the redistribution of wealth and benefits to the poor", and see what the speaker or author intends it to mean.

Another word of dubious integrity much loved by Socialists is 'fair', as in, "it's not fair that the rich enjoy benefits and advantages that the poor don't." The word 'fair', as we know, means "treated or regarded equally, without favouritism or discrimination". Synonyms are 'just', 'equitable', and 'reasonable'. 'Fair', however, is often the preferred synonym for statements of a moral nature. The reason for this is that while the synonyms 'just', 'equitable', and 'reasonable' appeal directly and explicitly to *reason* as the standard by which an issue under discussion should be judged, 'fair' is frequently used to appeal rather to the *emotions*. While all four synonyms share the judicial meaning of "treated or regarded equally, without favouritism or discrimination", 'fair' also has another, moral meaning; which the other synonyms do not share explicitly; where 'fair' means "morally right".

When in the course of a discussion someone says "It's not reasonable (or just, or equitable) that...." they are, because of the judicial nature of the word used, implicitly inviting reasoned consideration of their opinion. When, on the other hand, someone says "It's not fair that...." they are invariably not inviting anyone's reasoned consideration but are presenting a negative moral judgment as a fact. This emotionally charged usage plays on the alternative judicial and temperate meaning of 'fair' to acquire a credibility which the moral judgment does not necessarily warrant. The use by anybody of the phrase "It's not fair that...." serves as fair warning that in all probability an emotional value judgment is about to be passed off as an appeal to reason.

3.10 Altruism and Egoism

All the various forms of Socialism are characterised by their opposition to Capitalism and the free market, which they accuse of being basely motivated by egoism and greed, and lacking sufficient concern for the welfare of the less fortunate. The Socialists, on the other hand, claim to be motivated not just by self-interest, but principally by altruism – the desire to do good for others. The question as to whether this is indeed so needs to be examined.

We start by considering the fundamental biological fact that all humans are essentially self-interested, meaning that each individual's own survival and interest are the principal factors driving them biologically. This is not to say that the individual lacks feelings of altruism in respect of others, but simply that self-interest is their primary biological drive. This is clearly illustrated by the fact that it is into our own bank accounts that we deposit our monthly salary; ourselves that we feed daily, and our own teeth that we brush; not our neighbour's. This is the way that nature works, so far as we humans and most other animals are concerned, and in the struggle for survival, self-interest is a highly successful biological mechanism.

While humans are predominantly self-interested, we are not exclusively so. As social animals, concern for the welfare of others, and above all for those related to us, is biologically advantageous to our species and accommodated accordingly by our natures. In general, however, our altruistic tendencies are decidedly subordinate to our self-interest and, given that altruism and self-interest are contradictory behavioural mechanisms, it is easy to understand why this is so. An individual who dedicated most of their energy to furthering the interests of other individuals, rather than their own, would not be likely to survive long enough to do much good at all. Altruism obviously cannot be a primary drive. Although altruism and self-interest work in contradictory ways, one furthering the interests of the individual and the other those of the community, they are nevertheless complementary. Jointly they contribute to the survival of both the individual and the species, or community.

It is currently impossible to measure accurately our respective human predispositions toward self-interest and altruism, in order to ascertain just how self-interested and how altruistic the average human being actually is, and therefore may be expected to be in regard to their behaviour concerning collective, social matters, such as economic and political affairs. The church's call for tithing, the voluntary donation of 10% of one's income to charity, might arbitrarily be taken as a very rough guide to altruistic behaviour, suggesting that the average person might be considered to be approximately 90% self-interested and 10% altruistic. *Certainly, there must be very few people who voluntarily give away more than 10% of their incomes to strangers on a regular basis.* (In this regard, it might be helpful if you examine your own behaviour in order to establish just how much or your own time and money is spent serving the interests of strangers, to help give you an idea of just how altruistic you think the average person might be).

The relevance of this consideration lies in our attempting to establish just what degree of altruistic human behaviour might be considered to be reasonable in regard to how we treat other people's interests. Any such conception needs to relate to the real world, to how human beings are *actually* constituted and behave, rather than to how they *ought to* behave in accordance with some individual's subjective, and possibly unnatural view of human nature. Altruism is, after all, simply a biological behavioural trait, and not some mystical moral force.

A look at actual human behaviour over recorded time suggests that our predisposition to assist and support others plays a very secondary role to our self-interest, and is largely in proportion to their emotional proximity to us. We are generally prepared to do a great deal for those genetically close to us, a lot for our friends and clan, a bit for the nation, but very little for strangers. There are certain individuals who do far more for others than is generally the case, of course, but there are also those who do much less.

It is what is normal for humans to do for strangers that is relevant in arriving at reasonable social expectations, and not the extremes. Altruism is certainly an important consideration in terms of human social relationships that should be encouraged, but there is nothing to suggest that humans on average are sufficiently altruistic by nature to justify anything like the material claims made upon the individual in the name of altruism by Socialist redistributionist theory. On the contrary, in fact. Any study of human behaviour, present or past, reveals us to be decidedly unaltruistic in general, while capable at times of individual acts of kindness. The socialistic demands made of society in the name of altruism are totally disproportionate to the actual prevalence of altruism in human nature. If altruism exists in humans to the degree where, on average, they each regularly and voluntarily give no more than about 10% of their income or effort to strangers (and this figure is very likely on the high side), then it is irrational to demand anything more than this of society. Socialism, however, deliberately selects what is no more than a secondary human behavioural trait, and moralising and inflating it, claims by implication that in Socialists altruism is an as strong or even stronger impulse than self-interest, and should be so for all of society. Once again turning an 'ought' into an 'is', it then uses altruism as the excuse to justify its morally-engineered extortion from the economically most productive element in society.

Socialism uses its aggressive moral stance on equality to give the impression that it is a movement primarily concerned with helping the poor and doing good in the world. There is, however, no evidence to suggest that Socialism's political leaders or its adherents as individuals are any different to non-Socialists in regard to the degree of their personal altruistic behaviour. The socialist claim to be altruistically motivated, rather than self-interestedly, is therefore highly questionable. There is no doubt, however, that as political propaganda Sentimental Socialism is extremely successful, the public naively tending to take the politicians at their word. If Socialists, in general, are not *in practice*, as opposed to in theory, more altruistic than non-socialists, however, (and no evidence has ever been offered to prove that they are) then the claimed moral motivation for Socialism's coercive redistributionist policies is clearly nothing but morally pretentious fraud.

From an ideal viewpoint, there is much that could be said to be wrong with the world: injustice, greed, violence, poverty, selfishness, and exploitation, are rampant, among many other negative conditions. It is perfectly understandable that any decent person should protest against these on ethical grounds, and wish that they would change for the better. That it claims to undertake to do so is Socialism's great attraction for many people. The problem in attaining Utopia, however, is that these negative factors are not unique to Socialism's ideological opponents, Capitalism and the free market, as Socialism generally asserts, but are characteristic of human nature itself. Marxist and Socialist societies are hardly an improvement on capitalist ones. In fact, the contrary is generally true. Whatever political or economic system prevails, as history has shown us, there is always much that is wrong with society. Societies change, but human nature, at a fundamental level, does not. Socialism, after taking the very secondary human biological drive of altruism and inflating it politically to a theoretical position of primary importance, above natural self-interest, then makes the biologically questionable claim of being motivated itself principally by altruism, and only secondarily by self-interest.

Each society has its own way of assisting those who, for reasons beyond their control, are unable to support themselves. Traditionally, this support has always been given on a voluntary and genuinely altruistic basis. That it should be voluntary is rational, given that altruism is not the principal driving force in humans. Attempting to compel people to act against their inherent natures, as Socialism does, when it projects altruism as the primary issue in political discourse, is nothing but social engineering. The pseudo-democratic, coercive, redistributive system advocated and applied today is not a rational solution to the problem of relative poverty. It is not even a genuine, altruistically motivated attempt to assist the poor, but rather a deliberately contrived manipulation of public moral sentiment, specifically designed to win the electoral support that ideologues and the predatory elite need to attain their self-serving objectives, while at the same time pretending to be dedicated principally to helping the poor.

CHAPTER 4

Moral Law, Natural Law, and Democracy

4.1 Moral Law

Morality, as we have seen, is made up by, and consists in, human opinion. On each moral issue in each community there are likely to be numerous different individual and group opinions. While every individual is entitled to hold his or her own moral opinion on any particular issue, in order for any particular moral opinion to come to actually influence the general behaviour of the members of a community, it must be accepted as desirable and legitimate by everybody, or virtually everybody, in the community. Without this consensus, and with instead, a possibly conflicting multiplicity of moral opinions in a community, morality would have little utility. The function of morality ultimately is to positively affect the behaviour of all the members of a community, so that they all behave in a way consistent with the community's collective interest.

If what starts out as a simple moral opinion, does in due course come to achieve universal acceptance in a community, and so to influence the general behaviour, it is then elevated within the community to what we may refer to as Moral Law, whereupon it generally becomes accepted as binding on all members of the community. A Moral Law, then, is a moral belief or prescription which is accepted as legitimate and binding by all, or virtually all, members of any particular community.

Those moral beliefs that come to be regarded as Moral Law will not necessarily be identical in each community. The differing circumstances of each community will frequently produce local differences in what is held to be Moral Law. The varying moral attitudes in different communities regarding divorce, abortion, homosexuality, circumcision, and meat-eating, among others, illustrate this fact.

The greater the communal consensus on any particular moral belief, the greater will be its moral legitimacy and its effect on collective behaviour within the community. To illustrate; nearly every individual alive in every community on earth would presumably agree that murder and stealing are morally wrong. Prohibition against murder and stealing will therefore constitute Moral Law in all communities. On the other hand, divorce is morally acceptable in some communities but is unacceptable in others. In those communities where it is either universally accepted *or* rejected, the respective collective moral opinions on the issue in each community may be held to be Moral Law within the community. In those communities where there is no near-universal consensus on the matter either way, it cannot be held to be Moral Law, but remains simply individual or sectarian moral opinion. Morality is made, and can only be made, by consensus. And this is not for any mystical reason, but simply for the practical reason that if everybody in a community does not voluntarily accept the legitimacy or authority of a particular moral belief, they will not modify their behaviour to conform to it and the belief's utility will be nil.

It is expected that every reasonable person in each community will naturally agree with the moral rules and beliefs that come to constitute a community's moral code, because they view their implementation as necessary and acceptable, and desirable for their own well-being.

4.2 Natural Law

Those Moral Laws that are so widely recognised as being legitimate as to be common to all communities within a culture, may be regarded as Natural Laws. A Natural Law, then, is a moral belief which is accepted as self-evidently true by everybody, or virtually everybody, within a culture, or possibly even on earth. It is perceived to be inherent in, and derived from, nature and our common humanity, and understood by reason. The common prescriptions against murder and stealing are examples of Natural Laws. The First Generation Human Rights may also be regarded as Natural Law in the West, but they are not necessarily held to be so elsewhere. The same logic of unanimity that underpins the concept of Moral Law, also underpins that of Natural Law.

To establish for oneself whether or not someone's opinion on a moral issue reflects Moral or Natural Law, or is merely their opinion, one has only to ask oneself whether that opinion is universally shared within a community or not. If not, it is mere opinion.

4.3 Moral Law and Natural Law as Conventions

The concepts of Moral Law and Natural Law are, of course, purely conceptual conventions; as, for that matter, are the concepts of Human Rights, the Equality of Man, and Democracy itself. These things do not exist of themselves. They only exist as a voluntary conceptual agreement, agreed to by a community in the general interest, and will cease to exist once they are no longer agreed upon. Anyone is free to deny that they conform to reality. Unless the critics are nihilist, however, it is incumbent upon them to provide an alternative, rational, and moral paradigm that satisfactorily encompasses and explains the undeniable reality of human moral behaviour underpinning them.

4.4 The Unanimity Principle

It is difficult to see how the degree of consensus that is required in order to create effective Moral and Natural Law within a rationally organised community could be anything less than unanimous, or near-unanimous. The exact point at which simple moral opinion evolves for practical purposes into Moral or Natural Law or at which the unanimity principle kicks in, obviously cannot be stated with any sort of certainty. Is it 98% of a population or more, or does 95% suffice? Unanimity, or near-unanimity, is, however, clearly essential, not for mystical or moral reasons, but for the practical reasons we have seen; if a moral belief does not generate sufficient support within a community to reach the critical mass of acceptance required to become Moral Law, it cannot effectively come to regulate the actual collective behaviour of the community, because not enough people will be observing it.

The unanimity principle sets the bar high. And it extends beyond the single question of morality, to the whole issue of political decision making. In any society there will always be a multiplicity of opinions on most issues, reflecting the diversity of human nature. In non--democratic societies which accept some form of minority rule, such as oligarchy, dictatorship, or monarchy, unanimity is of no special relevance when it comes to making political decisions. It is central, however, to decision making in a democratic society. On what rational principles should collective decision-making be organised in a society that has utterly rejected minority rule and embraced Democracy and the concept of moral equality? We shall shortly consider the possible alternatives, but unanimity is really the only rational way to *fully* legitimise any collective decision on a democratic basis.

If a society is serious about the principle of equality, as Democratic societies claim to be, then in the legal decision-making process, logically no law may be passed which unequally affects the interests of any citizens, without their voluntary agreement. In other words, all legislation must affect everybody equally to be legitimate, or, alternatively, must be accepted by everybody if it does not affect them equally. If all men are morally equal before the law, what could possibly justify legislation being passed by some that negatively affected the interests of other individuals, against their wishes? Unanimity is the only legitimate expression of equality in regard to decision making. The democratic principle of strict equality before the law is, however, clearly not one that is being observed in the legislative programmes of the Western nations that describe themselves as democratic. The coercive expropriation of wealth for the purposes of redistribution illustrates this fact.

Furthermore, any decision-making process that allows legally enforceable decisions affecting everybody to be made by anything less than the tacit agreement of every individual concerned, not only violates the democratic principle of equality, but potentially legitimises minority rule, because *in principle* it accepts that decisions enforceable on everyone may be made by less than everyone.

4.5 Alternative Concepts for Collective Decision Making

The terms Moral and Natural Law are widely used, frequently without any clear definition being obvious or provided. This is unfortunate, as being undefined they are sometimes used to justify irrational ends. We have, however, provided here, with the criterion of unanimity, a clear and coherent definition of Moral and Natural Law. And it is impossible to imagine a meaningful or rational definition of Moral or Natural Law that does not require the assent and agreement of all rational citizens before a simple moral opinion can qualify as such.

The same consideration applies to any collective political decision that a community is required to make. On what basis are such decisions to be made, if they are to be both legitimate and peaceful? And specifically, on what basis should they be made in a society that has come finally to accept the principles that underlie Democracy? If everyone does not agree on any issue, there are obviously going to be conflicting views, and what gives any individual, or group of individuals, the moral right to make decisions affecting the Human Rights of others, without their agreement? Collective political decisions cannot be made with any moral authority by a minority, because on what moral basis could a minority be permitted to decide for the majority? The excesses of monarchy and totalitarianism have totally discredited minority rule in Western eyes. One perceived solution to this problem that many people subscribe to is majoritarianism – the sovereignty of the majority of the people in a community over the minority. Majoritarianism is held by many to give proper expression to the democratic principles of the moral equality of all men and of their equality before the law. Let us consider how valid this claim is.

4.6 The Nature of a Majority

It is widely believed that within the concept of Democracy there is some sort of moral virtue inherent in the majority of a number of people, as opposed to the minority; that the majority possesses a particular kind of moral authority or moral right, by virtue of being the larger of two portions. There is, however, no perceivable rational justification for this occult belief. The sole rational virtue of a majority is numerical, in so far as it is the most logical way of breaking a voting deadlock when two or more parties cannot come to agreement on some issue. And it is solely for this practical reason that the process of deciding an issue by means of majority vote in any vote or ballot was accepted in the democratic West as the means of arriving at a decision acceptable to all parties, by previous agreement. The concept of majority rule is a convention in its own right, and it has nothing to do with the democratic principle of equality, and the act of winning a vote by being in the majority does not confer any moral authority whatsoever on the winner that the loser does not equally possess.

The abstract concept of the moral equality of all men is a conceptual convention to which all reasonable and democratic Westerners presumably subscribe. As we have seen, the concept establishes that no person is to be regarded as morally superior to any other, and it also asserts that everybody is therefore to be held and treated as morally equal, and so as all possessing the same inherent Human Rights. Particularly, in the light of what had happened under the monarchy, all were to be equal before the law.

The concept of moral equality cannot therefore logically allow two people collectively a greater moral right than any single individual possesses. *The individual's moral rights are inherent in the individual themselves, and independent of all other individuals.* In terms of the democratic equality principle, for example, the fact that ten people have the right of free speech does not give them collectively a greater right to free speech than any single other individual, or the authority to deny that right to anyone else. Such a phenomenon would violate the very concept of equality. This fact raises the question as to the moral legitimacy in a Democracy of legislation being passed on the basis of a majority decision, *when such legislation does not apply equally to all parties, or discriminates against the interests of some.* If the numerical majority in a putatively democratic community may pass laws that negatively affect the interests of a minority, and are not supported by that minority, which is exactly what has been happening in the West since the 18th century, what gives them the moral right to do so?

4.7 Why Majority Rule is Undemocratic

The practice of decision-making on a majoritarian basis, common in supposedly democratic legislatures throughout the West today, in reality has nothing to do with either morality or equality. Putting two people together numerically, as we noted, cannot in any way increase their moral status or their Human Rights, relative to those of a single person. A concept that holds that the opinion or vote of any numerical majority in a community morally outweighs the opposing opinion of any minority violates the fundamental principle of the inherent moral equality of everybody. It also renders the moral system of equality before the law on which Democracy is based, incoherent.

Furthermore, if a numerical majority is allowed the moral authority to pass legislation that negatively affects the interests of a minority, and to which the minority is opposed, there is nothing to stop the majority from legitimately legislating against the minority's interests to the point where the minority can no longer survive. Accordingly, it would not be rational for any minority to enter into such an unequal and unprotected arrangement, quite apart from the fact that it violates the principle of moral equality, by subjecting some men to the arbitrary rule of others.

A majority in electoral terms, as we have noted, is simply a utilitarian electoral convention, agreed to by all parties, for arriving at a decision on a vote, by awarding it to the majority party. On winning a vote which passes a particular piece of legislation, the winning party gains nothing other than having the legislation become law. This is consistent with the concept of Democracy *so long as the legislation being voted upon does not discriminate against or for anyone's interests, so violating the democratic principle of equality and, specifically, that of equality before the law.*

That a simple majority decision is acknowledged to fall short of possessing full moral authority is indicated by the common requirement for an increased two-thirds or three-quarter majority in respect of major decisions, such as amending a constitution. This requirement is seen as enhancing the moral legitimacy of a simple majority decision, but inasmuch as a majority cannot rationally possess any moral authority over a minority in the first place, increasing a majority from 51% to 66% cannot possibly make any difference. Only the unanimity that is implicit in equal and unprejudicial treatment can provide moral authority. The widespread belief that a two-thirds majority confers greater moral authority than a simple majority indicates that many people mistakenly believe that the equality that Democracy demands is provided by majority voting, rather than in its fundamental requirement that everybody be treated equally in respect of all legislation, and nobody be discriminated against.

At times it is desirable to pass legislation which discriminates between the population at large and a minority group within it, for the common benefit. The prohibition against driving a motor vehicle before attaining a certain age is an example of this. Such instances of discrimination are permissible in terms of democratic principle, however, only because, and only as long as, they comply with the unanimity principle; namely, they apply to everybody equally, even if not necessarily at the same time.

The simple electoral procedure of deciding elections or ballots on the basis of which party gains the majority of votes is, we suggest, more accurately described as majority *voting*, rather than as majority *rule*. Majority *rule*, on the other hand, permits discrimination against minorities in its legislation, and this is why majority rule is undemocratic. Majority *rule* better describes the anti-democratic political practice common in the Western legislatures today which permits the party gaining the majority of votes to pass legislation which does not apply equally to everybody, and which may discriminate negatively against the interests of a minority. Progressive taxation for the purpose of redistribution, which compels those who earn more money, to pay tax at a higher rate, and so discriminates prejudicially against them, is an example of this practice. Inasmuch as under majority rule the majority may legally out-vote and override the objections of any minority, the majority may fairly be said to rule the minority.

If one accepts the principle of the moral equality of all men, it is a contradiction to believe that a majority has any right to rule over the minority. The majority has no more moral right to *rule* anybody than does any minority. The principle of the equality of man explicitly denies the majority any such right. Genuine Democracy is not majority rule. It is the rule of all the people by all the people, with equal treatment for all. Majority rule is not democratic, and the term is a misnomer when it is used as though it were synonymous with Democracy. Flatly, if Democracy does not mean that all men are to be treated equally, and that none may be discriminated against in any way, including in terms of legislation, then it is not rule of the people by the people. Nor does it give expression to the principle of the equality of man before the law. After all, this was the whole point of the democratic revolutions of the 18th century. It was certainly not the democratic intention to replace the tyranny of the aristocratic minority with the tyranny of the electoral majority. Any political system based upon the *rule* of the majority, which gives the numerical majority the right to legislate *without full and equal regard for the interests of the minority*, cannot coherently be based upon the concept of the equality of man before the law, because it flatly violates it.

So-called democratic political parties have all along chosen deliberately to behave as though majority rule fully complied with all the requirements of a democratic form of government, and was synonymous with it. Majority rule has, in fact, even been presented as the very hallmark of Democracy. The fundamental democratic requirements that all legislation should apply equally to everybody, and that nobody should discriminated against, were quietly ignored, while dramatic lip service was paid to the outer trappings of Democracy. Government in the West has never been conducted on the democratic principle of the equality of man, but rather on the practice of majority rule. And what is the *moral principle* underlying majority rule? There is none. As we have seen, there is no legitimate *moral* principle to be found in the concept of majority rule. It is simply a utilitarian convention for deciding votes and ballots. It is the shadow presented as the substance.

It is the politicians who, above all, have deliberately misinterpreted majority rule to mean Democracy. They are the people who operate and interpret the political system at all times and who benefit most directly from it. A political system run truly on the basis of democratic equality would present a greatly diminished opportunity, both for them and for those who use them to attain their own ends. If all men are truly to be held equal before the law, then, as we have seen, no person may be discriminated against in respect of any legislation without his agreement. This fact, in turn, means that the only legislation that could ever be passed would be that which was considered to be in their own interests by every citizen – i.e. legislation that complied with the unanimity principle, and was clearly perceived to be equally in everyone's interests, *just as what qualify as moral laws in any society are only those that everybody agrees with.* This democratic requirement would greatly inhibit the politicians and the dominant element which always controls society from doing so through legislation, as the only laws that could ever be passed would be those that everybody agreed with. The State would be likely to be very much smaller than it is today, and performing far fewer functions. This is exactly how it should be, many will say: the State has already swollen out of all reasonable proportion, taking on a life of its own, at the expense of individual initiative and freedom. It would also be impossible to have the laws that served the special interests of only portions of society passed, unless everyone could be persuaded to agree with them. This would severely limit the ability of society's dominant elite to control and manipulate it. Which is really how it should be, in terms of democratic principles. That is the whole point of Democracy; to prevent a minority, or minorities, from dominating the *demos*, the people.

Accordingly, the controlling elite in effect saw to it that the genuinely democratic concept of equality before the law that the anti-monarchical revolutions had reactively thrown up was quietly buried, and then reincarnated in the form of majority rule, purporting to be synonymous. Thus did Western society pass from one form of minority rule, monarchy, to another form, oligarchy, with only a theoretical stop at genuine Democracy on the way.

It may be asked why it is important for us in the modern, secular world to organise ourselves politically on a genuinely moral basis, such as genuine Democracy offers. The answer is simply that if we do not all agree that government should be conducted on the basis of rational and mutually accepted moral principles, then it will be conducted with scant regard for any rational moral principles at all, and power will, as it has always done, fall duly into the hands of the strong and the manipulative. This is what has been happening since the 18th century revolutions. While the West professes to be democratic, it has practised majority rule instead of Democracy, and majority rule is effectively no more than Newspeak for minority rule.

It will be argued forcefully that this analysis of the fallacy underlying majority rule may be accurate, but the reality is that this is how the modern world is, and has to be, run; that government operating on the principle of unanimity just would not be practical. This, of course, might be true, but not necessarily so. If something as complex and as subtle as morality is spontaneously formulated and applied in each community on the basis of unanimity, why should general legislation not also be? But even if it cannot, this does not alter the fact that the practice of majority *rule* contradicts the fundamental moral and political principles of equality upon which Democracy is supposedly based, and *if these democratic principles are as important as we have all along been saying that they are*, there are likely to be major negative consequences for this contradiction, some of which we are possibly witnessing now, and more of which we are likely to see in the future. Should violating the principle of equality before the law have no negative consequences, well and good. If this proves to be so, however, it means that all we have been taught about the benefits of Democracy was untrue. Is this likely? This is not a call for genuine Democracy; merely a warning that if the political and moral logic underlying Democracy is important, and if it is ignored or twisted, there will inevitably be unfortunate consequences for all of us.

To violate the principle of equality by practising majority rule invites the very consequences that the concept of Democracy and the principle of equality were specifically designed to avoid. The most egregious of these negative consequences was the historical domination and control of society by one predatory minority or the other. The ongoing manipulation of Western society by powerful minority interest groups, commercial, financial, and other, illustrates this. For a number of reasons, genuine Democracy based on unanimity may be impractical, but we should not delude ourselves that anything less will not be likely to exact a high cost in terms of social corruption and lost individual freedom, among other things. By the latter is meant the ability of the individual to live with a minimum of interference by the State and others in their private life. The further that governance moves from genuine Democracy in practice, the greater the demands of the State and the loss of individual freedom are likely to be.

The specific danger that majority rule brings, is that it openly permits legislation to be passed and implemented that either favours a minority or special interest over the community as a whole, or disfavours a minority. All that is generally required for this to happen, is for a number of the influential elected representatives to be persuaded that it is very much in their personal interests to support a particular piece of legislation, and for sufficient money to be provided for them to purchase the necessary support and assistance. No obvious conflict with the interests of their constituents need arise. The relatively small number of elected representatives in legislatures, and the highly profitable returns obtainable from remunerating them financially and otherwise, makes corruption inevitable and endemic under majority rule. And corruption is an integral part of majority rule, because it was specifically designed to allow the new, middle-class predatory elite to keep their new-found control of post-aristocratic society, while assuring the masses that with Democracy their day had finally come. The morally based principles upon which genuine Democracy was founded take the questionable and erratic nature of human beings fully into account. Not being based upon any principles, however, moral or otherwise, majority rule leaves the sheepfold gate wide open to the wolves.

The 18th century Democratic revolutions were bourgeois revolutions. Having wrested power and authority from the aristocracy, the bourgeoisie were never going to hand it to the peasantry. Having rallied opposition to the aristocracy with the universal slogan of "Liberty, Fraternity, and Equality", however, they could not openly claim power for themselves. Instead, they shouted the slogan louder, and, quietly smothering the infant Democracy, proudly presented its bastard sibling, Majority Rule, to the cheering masses.

4.8 Democracy and Pseudo-Democracy: The Corrupted State

Democracy is a rational form of secular government, based upon the strict application of the principles of the moral equality of man and the First Generation Human Rights, whereby no legislation may be passed which discriminates unfavourably against the interests of any minority in society, without its agreement. No such government has ever existed in the West in practice.

Pseudo-Democracy is the form of government simulating Democracy, which pretends to be based on the above, but which practises majority rule, and is based on superstition inasmuch as it accepts that moral opinion can be fact and that morality is objective, and therefore is not created solely by mankind. It presents itself as democratic in order to flatter the masses and lead them to believe that it exists principally in order to further their interests. All the main political parties in the West today, regardless of whether they describe themselves as conservative, progressive, humanist, nationalist, liberal, democratic, social-democratic, or socialist, are essentially pseudo-democratic. Presenting themselves as representatives of the people, it becomes increasingly clear that they have to a large extent been captured by powerful special interests. They finance themselves, as politicians have always done, by redistributing the wealth in society from those who are currently generating it to the politically influential individuals who are not, redistributing a sufficiency to themselves. Like the kings, popes, and pharaohs of old, they justify their role in society by claiming to be essential to its wellbeing. They are, in reality, often the principal cause of its misfortunes.

The redistribution of wealth, rather than its creation, is the principal element in pseudo-democracy's economic policy. While coercive wealth redistribution presents itself, and is widely believed to be, a moral way of resolving the problem of relative poverty in society, in fact, over the long run, coercive wealth redistribution not only fails to benefit the poor as a class, but corrupts the whole of society, including the poor. It corrupts society as a whole by legitimising irrationality and by compromising society's moral standards. Theft by the State is presented, Robin Hood-like, as a virtue, provided that it is undertaken to promote the mystical cause of what is ambiguously described as Social Justice. With this moral sleight-of-hand, rationality is abandoned, public morality is inverted, and the gates opened to any irrational claims made in the name of social justice that can win sufficient popular support.

On what grounds can anyone resist *any* claim made against them in the name of social justice, once rationality has been abandoned and the mystical concept has been widely accepted in society as a meaningful and legitimate governing principle – as has happened today? And how can moral standards possibly be maintained in a society that deliberately legitimises selective theft by the State; where one portion of the people openly connives against another, and where the logical and moral connection between work and material reward is consciously broken?

Among the principal victims of wealth redistribution, however, are the poor, the very people that its implementation claims to benefit. They are particularly corrupted by being turned into a permanent and dependent underclass. Rather than aiming at eliminating relative poverty by eliminating its root causes, wealth redistribution perpetuates it. Because the real object of redistribution is not to assist the poor, but to provide the political hierarchy with an ongoing excuse for tapping into the wealth of the economically most productive, the so-called solution to the problem of the poor is of necessity also viewed in an ongoing light. So instead of regarding the poverty of individuals as a temporary condition, which is to be remedied by the facilitation of the work opportunities that they each require in order to be able to lift themselves out of poverty, their relative poverty is by and large regarded as permanent. They are accordingly bought off by the State, not by the creation of an environment conducive to their reemployment, but with a subsidised income. This, of course, apart from buying their political support, provides them with a strong incentive not to seek work, and so their condition becomes permanent, and so, degrading. The poor are being used as an excuse to redistribute income, some of which filters through to them, but the major part of which goes to other beneficiaries.

Above all, the disproportionate tax extorted from the wealthy allows the State and its bureaucracy to grow far beyond the point that it would be able to if the majority of the electorate had to bear the financial cost of its benefits themselves. There is nothing, short of financial collapse, to stop the State from growing incessantly, once politicians are able to offer the electorate benefits which the electorate do not expect to have to pay for personally. Furthermore, the practice of progressive taxation, which is supposedly there to ensure that the wealthy pay more tax than those earning less, while generally achieving this, also allows the State to tax middle-class citizens, who are far from 'wealthy', more, because the progressive taxation starts at a relatively low point. The knowledge that the wealthy are taxed at a higher rate, however, makes the absurdly high tax rate that those in the middle income brackets are suffering, somehow more acceptable to them.

The metastasised bureaucratic State, invariably heavily in debt incurred to pay for ever-more exotic benefits for the voters, remote from the functioning of the actual market, obsessed by regulation, which provides its bureaucrats with the illusion of controlling circumstances, encumbers the natural economic productivity of the open-market economy that the poor in the first place depend completely upon for their economic upliftment. As history has repeatedly shown, *it is entrepreneurial productivity in the open market, utilising saved capital, that generates the real wealth that benefits the poor and society as a whole, and not the moralistic and second-hand redistribution of already- created wealth.* If long-term assistance for the poor is anyone's genuine objective, they cannot rationally support the expropriation of wealth from society's most economically productive members, its passage through the prodigal hands of the ever-growing, middle-class bureaucracy, and the transference of the residue to an economically passive underclass that does not produce, but only consumes. Only gross delusion could accommodate the belief that such a programme actually benefits the poor in the medium and long-term. And only wilful blindness or economic illiteracy could prevent anyone from seeing the harm that is being done to society as a whole by Socialism's anti-rational, corrupting, atavistic, and occult moralism. As bread and circuses were the symptoms of Rome's decline, so the Welfare State is symptomatic of ours.

Quite apart from its practice of the expropriation and redistribution of wealth, the principal Western political system of majority rule is deeply corrupt in itself, being based as it is upon the lie that it is morally motivated and is dedicated to giving expression to the principle of the equality of all men. What chance is there for a society to operate on a rational and moral basis when it rests on so incoherent and questionable a foundation?

4.9 Democracy or Oligarchy?

It is surely significant that throughout its history the West has *always* been governed by one or the other form of minority rule, of which monarchy, dictatorship, and oligarchy seem to have been the most popular. In Ancient Greece and Republican Rome, the brief interludes of apparent Democracy were not exceptions, as they were effectively slave-owning oligarchies with male-only, qualified franchises, rather than Democracies as we understand the word today. The essential element that distinguishes our modern conception of Democracy and its attendant Human Rights from the ancient versions, is the former's conceptual origin as lying in our very humanity, and its consequential extension to every living human being. For the Athenians and the Republican Romans, only the property-owning, male citizens of particular communities were perceived to possess the inherent qualities necessary to be able to beneficially and significantly form part of democratic society, and it was from these particular qualities that their democratic nature and their Human Rights were held to arise. And today's majority rule, pseudo-Democracy, is not an exception, for the reasons we have given, although many fondly, but misguidedly, regard it as such. In reality, it is a form of oligarchy dressed as Democracy, but failing in Democracy's fundamental requirement – to treat all men equally before the law.

If mankind has always been governed by one form or the other of minority rule, as appears to be the case, perhaps this is how we are actually biologically predisposed to be governed, and the genuinely democratic concept of equality is an unrealisable anomaly, an intellectual and moral quirk that our primitive biological natures are unable to accept. This could be why the genuine concept of equality has everywhere and by everyone today been reinterpreted rather to mean majority rule. In the light of our past history, it is, perhaps, excessively naive to believe that we can ever govern ourselves in a genuinely democratic manner. Should we elect to do so, however, it would have to be organised and based solely upon rational principles, and not the superstitious, faith-based ideologies that currently dominate our intellectual and political horizons, and which have always been used to rationalise the past forms of minority rule. Unanimity would be its hallmark.

Looking back over history, it is clear that the majority is not inclined to rule itself, and may well not even be capable of doing so. Democracy, as the effective rule of all by all, therefore appears to be an inappropriate form of human government. As social animals, hierarchically ordered, we are seemingly not qualified for genuine Democracy, and majority rule is no more than a political system that has evolved in order to allow those who are capable of working their way to the top of the social hierarchy to retain control of society, while paying lip-service to the radical, naive, and supremely rational principle of Democracy. This is not a happy conclusion from a genuinely democratic perspective.

CHAPTER 5

Further Considerations

5.1 Racism and Common Sense

One of the major problems in the world today – racism – is a prime example of the harm that is done to society when moral opinion is accepted as fact: specifically, in the case of racism, when the moral opinion of the relatively uneducated – namely, that members of another race are biologically inferior - is taken to be a fact. Racism is unequivocally wrong in today's moral terms. It is not a moral *fact* that racism is wrong, however, as we now know; it is rather the predominant, current moral *opinion* in the West that it is. And the significance of this very important distinction lies in the two very different ways that the problem is likely to be dealt with in order to try to resolve it, using each of the two respective attitudes.

As with slavery, for by far the greater part of recorded human history, racism was viewed in a quite different light to that common today, in that it was accepted as normal in all societies. And there was a good reason for this. Humans in general fear, or are uncomfortable with, whatever appears to be significantly different to what they are accustomed to, for fear that it might harm them or their interests. Discrimination (and racism is but one of its many forms) is a form of defence against the potential threat presented by what is different to what we are familiar with. The inherent and powerful dislike and suspicion of difference is in all probability an ancient biological adaptation to what has invariably been a hazardous environment for mankind, where for hundreds of thousands of years of its existence, 'different' potentially meant 'deadly'. Race, as the perceived division of mankind based upon distinct, shared physical characteristics, was a strong marker of potential difference, and in the past particularly of cultural and behavioural difference.

The generally negative feelings prompted in someone by what we call racism are directed at more than simply the race of the victim. Race, as identified by physical appearance, such as skin colour and facial configuration, is the most vivid and immediately identifiable marker of potential difference, but the negative feelings typical of racism are aroused by other, more significant but less readily visible differences, such as those of culture, custom, and beliefs. The real, underlying problem is not an aversion to racial difference in itself, but our deep, inherent, and quite natural aversion to whatever we are not familiar with and accustomed to: to whatever presents a potential threat to our safety and wellbeing.

In coming to an understanding of what racism really is, it needs to be remembered that racial prejudice was the approved social norm until *as recently as the mid-twentieth century.* It would be more logical to ask why racism is held to be wrong today than why it was held to be right previously. And it would be extremely naive to believe that Western society has so recently become strongly anti-racist because we have somehow become morally superior to our ancestors. The fact that racism has recently become morally unacceptable in the West is not the result of some sudden moral enlightenment, but is principally the eventual outcome of the vast migrations and mixing of peoples that took place across the world during the 19th and 20th centuries, the migrations themselves being a consequence of the earlier 18th century Industrial Revolution. These not only shattered the comfortable cultural homogeneity of the agrarian Western societies, but were also contemporaneous with the spread of the universal franchise in the industrialising West. Relatively suddenly, after countless millennia of being a socially beneficial factor for the relatively small communities in which mankind had up to that time lived, racism ceased to be so in the new, larger, and increasingly racially mixed industrial societies which came to replace them. On the contrary, from the mid-20th century, racism became a major social problem. And it only became a problem because Western society had in the interim become multiracial, and racism now divided the newly formed, multiracial societies from within rather than protecting them from without. While the changing social and political circumstances compelled the political leaders of the Western democracies by the mid-20th century to rethink and alter their attitudes in respect of racial and cultural difference, they were quite incapable of eliminating the deeply ingrained racial prejudice inherent in both themselves and society at large. This is the problem that we sit with today. In bringing about globalisation, ever-accelerating human technological and political development has far outpaced mankind's ancient, socially formed nature. Our intellect tells us that racial discrimination in multiracial societies is counterproductive and socially divisive, and so, now morally wrong, but our instinctive tribal memory compels us individually to continue to discriminate by judging people in terms of their appearances, for reasons that are by and large not nearly as relevant as they once were.

There is a school of politically-correct thought that seeks to solve the problem of racism by denying that such a thing as race exists biologically, maintaining that race is solely a social construct. As there is only one race biologically, they argue, and that is the human race, anyone who asserts that there are different races is wrong. And not only biologically wrong, but morally wrong as well, because implicit in the concept of races is the notion of superiority and inferiority. By closing down all discussion of race, on what is, in fact, a highly contentious issue in scientific circles, the problem of racism as a practical, social problem is thereby supposedly resolved. All that remains is to condemn all those who practise any form of racism as immoral.

This argument hinges on the definition chosen of 'race'. The common definition of race as the "major divisions of mankind having distinctive physical characteristics" refers, through the use of the word 'distinctive,' to *visible* physical characteristics, not to microscopic, DNA-level biological differences, and such major divisions clearly exist, as identified by the widely understood terms 'Caucasian, Oriental, and Negroid'. What the politically-correct school presumably means when it states that there is only one race, the human race, is that there is only one human *species* biologically at DNA level, which we all know to be true. There is indeed only one human species, but there are also several human races – defined as "the major divisions of mankind having distinct physical characteristics."

Whether or not such a classification as race exists biologically is anyway of little relevance in respect of the existence of racism. Defined as "negative prejudice directed against someone perceived to be of different race, as commonly understood" or otherwise, even those who deny that race exists do not deny the existence of racism. In this regard, the debate around the existence or non-existence of race is irrelevant and a deliberate red herring.

The moralising of racism, that is, treating its perceived wrongness as an objective moral fact, rather than as subjective moral opinion arising from changed historical and social circumstances, and piously accusing those guilty of it of being morally defective, and admonishing them to conform to the shiny, new moral standard, offers no solution to the problem, because it does not in any way address the root cause. Namely, the fact that the vast majority of humans can no more stop themselves from automatically responding to the difference that *they think* they detect in someone racially different to themselves than they can to anything else that might present a threat to them.

(If you have difficulty accepting this, test your own status in this regard by honestly and frankly assessing your own feelings in respect of members of races other than your own, with whom you come into regular contact. Are those feelings *identical* in every respect to the feelings that you have for members of your own race or ethnic group? Of course they are not, but that is what they would have to be for you, or for anybody else, to be able to claim honestly and unhypocritically that they are entirely free of all racial feelings and prejudice. Let us be frank, we are all racists in this respect, and our racism differs only in degree. This acknowledgement is the first step required to solve the problem.)

Any solution to the problem caused by racism in today's multiracial society lies, first, in understanding its real cause, and, secondly, in addressing this directly. Racism will only diminish or be eliminated when the fear and suspicion engendered in individuals and groups by the differences that they believe to be implicit in it, are reduced or eliminated through people's *practical* daily racial experiences. And, then, when the benefits of non-racism are made evident to everybody in *practical* ways. As the principal initiator and proponent of non-racialism, it is the State's responsibility to see that these two things happen.

Self-righteous and hypocritical moralising only exacerbates the problem by offering something as a solution that makes the problem even more difficult to solve. Nobody is ever going to be won over to non-racism by being told that they are morally defective. To solve the problem of racism it is necessary that both its nature and pervasiveness be acknowledged. Racism is not simply a moral problem, any more than murder is: socially, they are principally practical problems, requiring practical solutions. Does anyone believe that a lecture on the immorality of murder would in any way reduce the murder rate?

Morality exists specifically in order to assist mankind in solving *practical* social problems. Morality based upon superstition and mysticism, however, cannot do this because it does not deal in practicalities, but in moral fantasies. Racism is unequivocally morally wrong in terms of today's Western moral code, certainly, but the problem cannot be solved by cursing and throwing stones at the racists.

The moralists who throw accusations of racism around do so because they believe it to be an objective fact that racial prejudice is morally wrong. The racists who throw accusations of racial inferiority around do so because they believe it to be an objective fact that the members of another race are morally inferior. The racial moralist and the racist are bigoted birds of a feather.

5.2 Left Wing/Right Wing

The categorisation of people into left wing or right wing ostensibly expresses a difference in their political beliefs. The dichotomy is generally far wider than purely political, however, and may possibly reflect two very temporally different social philosophies, as suggested by Karl Popper, and possibly even two very different types of human character.

While the division between political left and right is understood to represent two opposites, this does not apply at the extremes: the extreme left and the extreme right tend to converge. If the normal political left and right are represented as the respective extremities of a horizontal bar (with Liberalism at the centre of the bar), the extreme left and extreme right are best represented by curving the bar into a circle, which brings the left and right together. The extreme left and the extreme right tend to be more similar than different. Rather than opposing each other philosophically, they, together, oppose Liberalism. This observation led Hitler to conclude that the Communists in Germany were the ideal potential converts to National Socialism – and vice versa. The similarity of the extremes also obscures the real differences between more 'normal' left-wing and right-wing beliefs, such as they might be. What follows is speculative. It also expresses strong, but healthy, prejudice, which should be appropriately adjusted for.

We are trying to understand why Socialists and others on the Left should be inclined to believe what they do, and, as far as we are able, why those on the Right sometimes believe differently.

In essence, as has been noted before by others, the characteristic left-wing viewpoint appears to represent that of the collective, of society as a whole. In contrast, the viewpoint characteristic of the Right, in so far as it differs from that of the Left, generally represents the viewpoint of the individual, and particularly when this is in conflict with the collective interest or opinion. Thus, in any potential conflict of interest, Socialists hold the interests of the collective to take precedence over those of the individual member of society. This inclination has certain consequences in terms of its application in the practical world. Firstly, leftists will tend to favour a larger role for the State in terms of social organisation, as opposed to the smaller, private initiative favoured by the right. The State is seen by the Left to be the embodiment of the community. Secondly, leftists will tend to favour the State as the provider of education, teaching what the State wishes to be taught. Thirdly, and most importantly, leftists resent and object to the distribution of wealth resulting from an economy organised on free-market principles. These principles are essentially individualistic, distributing material reward to each individual in accordance with the value that the other individuals operating in the market place upon the good or service that individual brings to the market. Most leftists favour the post facto, egalitarian *re*distribution by the State of a large portion of the privately produced wealth, after it has already been distributed along individualistic lines by the market, which suggests that they actually regard all wealth as the inherent moral property of the collective, even though it is very clearly not produced by the collective, but principally by individuals working in their own interests and at their own risk. The Left in general prefers a far greater role for the State in the economy: a total role, in fact, in respect of Communism.

The collective, of course, is made up of individual people. The question therefore arises, when their own interests come into conflict with those of the community, does the leftist individual favour the community's interests over their own, or not. This is an important question, because the answer would tell us whether the individual leftist is essentially motivated by either self-interest (if he will favour his own interests) or altruism (if he will favour the collective's). To put it metaphorically, do leftists brush each other's teeth, or do they brush only their own? Are they, contra nature, as individuals more *altruistic* than *self-interested*? Violating human nature, as it does, this possibility is highly unlikely, and there is no scientific evidence to suggest that leftists are any more altruistic in their actual personal behaviour than centrists, or rightists, as previously noted. On balance, they are unlikely to be more altruistic than anyone else. If they are not more altruistic, there is no reason to believe in any meaningful way that they do actually favour the collective's interests over the individual's in all instances. Perhaps they only favour the collective's interests over every individual's interests *other than their own*. If this is so, then possibly the leftist is not inherently pro-collective as such.

If they do actually favour their own personal interests over those of the collective when a conflict of interest arises, which seems likely, why do they otherwise favour the collective's interests over all other individual's interests? Could it possibly be because, as individuals, they lack the self-confidence required to see themselves readily in free competition with all other individuals, and so support the claims of the collective over those of other individuals in order to put the others at a competitive disadvantage relative to themselves? This is highly speculative, but why otherwise would an individual put the collective interests before those of other individuals like himself, given the fact that as individuals we are all considerably more self-interested in our behaviour than altruistic? Do leftists support the collective when it is in conflict with other individuals principally because they feel that they have more to fear from other individuals, than from the collective, which, as the repository of all communal values is hostile to individualistic challenge and conflict, and so a source of refuge and comfort for the timid and fearful?

Could it be, as Ludwig Von Mises suggests, that Capitalism and the free market present, not only the opportunity to succeed and gain relative status and wealth in one's community, but also the opportunity to fail, relative to one's peers? If one's social status in life is not fixed, or determined by factors beyond one's control, such as if one is born into the aristocracy or peasantry, but principally by one's own personal talent, ability, and effort, and there exist, as there always will, in one's own sphere of activity, those superior individuals who are wealthier or who have achieved more, is this not a source of acute displeasure to the ego of the average person, and a reason to loathe the economic system that encourages such difference? We do not generally resent the huge earnings of talented athletes, artists, or musicians, because their abilities are so far above the average that the question of any odious comparison with ourselves does not arise. (You can be sure, however, that among the members of each group it does.) Do leftists generally favour the collective over the individual because they individually lack the inherent self-confidence to enable them to happily face the challenge of free competition in all the spheres of life? Is this the psychological basis of egalitarianism and the desire for equality? Why else would anyone want everyone to be equal, and be so averse to difference?

In trying to understand why the Left is so obsessed specifically with the issue of material equality, a reason that suggests itself is that material inequality emphasises what can be interpreted as a clear *qualitative* difference between individuals in regard to the ability to earn money at least. Is the Left's desire for equality reflective of the 'Tall Poppy Syndrome' – an aversion to any measurable difference between people that might in any way suggest or imply that some are inherently better or morally superior to others? Clearly, there are in every society gifted individuals whose talent, intelligence, or determination exceeds the average. And it is generally these exceptional individuals who, through their ability or effort, have lifted mankind from the primitive level at which it would otherwise in all probability exist. Is the demand for equality perhaps nothing more than an expression of jealous resentment of such individuals?

It is highly unlikely that altruism or compassion satisfactorily explains the Left's obsession with rendering everyone equal, because genuine altruism or compassion would hardly accommodate the coercive expropriation of honestly earned property from innocent people required by wealth redistribution. And genuine altruism would anyway advocate upward rather than downward levelling.

In a sense, egalitarianism is a modern-day version of tribalism, where this incorporates communal ownership of the land. Each tribesman is free to grow or graze what he wishes on his allotment, but nobody is expected to become significantly wealthier than their neighbours. It is from this bucolic perception that the modern concept of equality possibly derives. The only affluence readily tolerated is the chief's, and that because he is representative of the whole community and so is expected to be seen as a 'Big Man'.

This subconscious bias perhaps also goes some way to explain why the Socialist propagandists fixed upon the irrational inequality allegation in the first place. In a primitive, agrarian social environment, equality (and relative poverty) is the natural state of affairs, and perhaps today's leftists, like Jean-Jacques Rousseau, are unconsciously and atavistically harking back to Utopian earlier times, when life was supposedly simpler and mankind is thought of as having been happier. This would also help explain the leftist aversion to globalisation and industrialisation, which are seen as symptomatic of individualistic Capitalism, and hostile to bucolic, Utopian Collectivism.

Another characteristic of the Left is its belief in the perfectibility of man, as opposed to the Liberal or Conservative belief that man is as he is and will always be so. Indicative of this belief is the leftist preference for 'nurture' rather than 'nature' as the explanation of the principal formative factor of human character. The idea that mankind is perfectible implies that he is born inherently imperfect in some way or other, and therefore requires the assistance of that leftist, intellectual elite in society that knows what is best for him, and will lead him to a higher state of being. The belief in the virtue and need for a moral and intellectual elite to lead mankind is also characteristic of the Left. This elite on occasion embarrassingly fails to conceal its contempt for the masses. (In regard to leadership, the Right evinces a distinct preference for dictators.)

The concept of perfectibility appears to be a basically religious one, introducing the modern version of the concept of original sin, with the all-knowing intellectual filling the role previously occupied by the church hierarchy. The belief in perfectibility explains the importance that the left places on the State controlling education, rather than society as a whole doing so. In terms of leftist theology, it is not only the individual who may be redeemed, but all of society itself, in the form of the Socialist State. We have seen the result of such redemption in the form taken by the Soviet Union from 1917.

Intellectuals appear frequently to be leftist in their political views. This, as Eric Hoffer suggests, is perhaps because the Left pays them more heed, employs them, and gives readier credence to their theories, where the Right generally despises them.

It has been suggested that the Left's deference to an intellectual elite represents a form of infantilism, a reversion to the safety and security of familial elders, who always know best.

While the leftist personality may reasonably be associated with the defining features mentioned above, it is not so easy to identify the rightist personality. It is easier to describe what the Right opposes than what it supports. Generally, but not always, it opposes a large State, and its increasing interference in people's lives. If it specifically supports anything, it could be said to be individual freedom and the interests of the individual over the collective. They also tend to be strong supporters of nationalism, as opposed to any form of internationalism, and with this, possibly a stronger inclination to racism, as a function of their nationalism. The relative lack of firm features distinguishing the Right compared to those on the Left, suggests perhaps that the Left may be the default position for humans, with the rightist character being anomalous. This would be consistent with the right-wing instinctive tendency to support the individual's interests over those of the collective. And, if most entrepreneurs and businessmen are rightist, perhaps the rightist is personally less risk-averse than the leftist.

This is all speculative, and there are many instances of collective human behaviour that seemingly combine left-wing and right-wing characteristics. Hitler's National Socialists, for example, were collectivist, Socialist, nationalist, *and* racist. We are unable, unfortunately, to say yet with any certainty why those on the Left or Right choose to believe what they do, but hopefully neuroscience will in due course tell us, once it has better data than those obtained from questionnaires.

5.3 The Paradox of our Ignorance

As laymen trying to decide for ourselves whether anthropogenic global warning does indeed threaten the planet or whether it doesn't, we have a major problem. Being neither statisticians nor climatologists nor otherwise fully expert in the subject, we are simply not competent to assess the accuracy, relevance, and significance of all the highly technical data that are presented as evidence by the opposing schools of climate science. This problem applies not only to global warming but to any relatively complex matter about which we are not expert or do not have first-hand experience: which is to say, it applies to most things that *we think* we know to be true and on which we have an opinion, but about which we actually know nothing or very little.

In order to understand the world around us, and survive in it, we require knowledge of it. This knowledge is obtained through the process of analysing sensory and intellectual data received and then separating it into the factual and the false. Here we immediately encounter a problem; how do we know which data is factual and which is false?

Each of us in the course of our lives tends to acquire a certain particular knowledge and expertise through the exercise of our principal occupation. A doctor will come to acquire significant medical knowledge, a carpenter that of wood and woodworking, a physicist of the material world, and so on. In addition, we obviously acquire other knowledge throughout the course of our lives, particularly regarding ourselves. Anyone's total knowledge of the world, however, no matter how brilliant or qualified they might be, is only ever a minute fraction of the sum total of knowledge currently shared among all of mankind. We nevertheless need to make our lifetime's way through an infinitely complex world. So how do we as individuals know, of all the data we receive over the course of our lives in respect of those areas in which we are not expert (i.e. virtually all of them0, what is true and what is untrue?

Do you know with absolute certainty whether man-caused global warming is taking place? - what causes inflation? – what the cause of the present economic crisis is? – whether plastics are causing mass infertility? - when the world will run out of oil? – whether capitalism is a good or bad thing? - how dangerous nuclear power really is? – if taking vitamin supplements is beneficial? To have any possible chance of answering any of these, or any other complex and contentious questions accurately, we obviously need to possess expert knowledge. If we personally lack such knowledge, as will nearly always be the case, we then have to rely on the opinion of somebody else who *is* expert on the subject and so does possess all the requisite knowledge. Furthermore, it needs to be someone who can also be relied upon to give us an accurate and objective answer, undistorted by his or her own prejudices and preconceptions. Only then can we be in a position to form any sort of rational opinion on the subject, with any chance of our opinion accurately reflecting reality, rather than our personal delusions.

As long as complex matters of fact are not contentious, and all experts are in general agreement, then we simply accept the consensual opinion as true, and so as our own. It is on the frequent occasions when matters of fact are disputed, however, and we are not expert that we are lost and unable to form an accurate and truthful opinion alone, and so require the opinion of experts to enable us to do so.

Unfortunately, relying on the opinion of experts is by no means guaranteed to assist us in arriving at the truth when any matters of fact are disputed by other experts. For lacking the relevant knowledge on a particular issue ourselves, how can we ever know for certain if our expert is actually correct in his opinion, regardless of how much we might respect him or wish to trust him? The lack of knowledge on our part that compels us to rely on expert opinion in the first place, simultaneously prevents us from being able to know for certain if our preferred expert is in fact correct in his assessment. Experts are wrong on occasion. Sometimes even, as history teaches us, *all* the experts on a particular subject prove to be wrong: the earth turned out to be round, after all. Furthermore, if a question is subject to dispute among experts, as is that of man-made global warming, clearly some of the experts must be wrong if the others are right. So how can we ever be certain that our preferred experts are in fact correct? We cannot, unfortunately, and are thus faced here with the paradox of our ignorance; *the personal ignorance that requires us in the first place to rely on expert opinion in order to form an intelligent opinion on a subject, equally prevents us from being able to assess whether the expert's opinion is actually accurate or not.*

We first encounter the paradox when we start to form an opinion on any disputed subject in which we are not expert but in which we are interested. After consideration, we generally choose to believe one particular expert opinion over the others, and duly make theirs our own opinion. In doing this, however, we implicitly dismiss as untrue or inaccurate the evidence and opinion of those experts whose opinions we do not accept, *even though our ignorance largely disqualifies us from making any such judgment rationally or meaningfully.* In matters in which we're not expert we're no more qualified to reject expert opinion than we are to affirm it. This is not what should be happening if we are serious about forming an opinion that accords as closely as possible with reality.

At the very least, reason suggests that we should suspend or severely curtail judgment in respect of any disputed complex question about which we cannot speak with proper authority or full knowledge. But we don't do this by and large. Rather, if the question has any interest for us at all, we appear to be keen to confirm the validity of the viewpoint which has the greatest emotional appeal to us, and to disparage any opposing viewpoints. We are inclined to be partisan rather than objective. It appears that our purpose in supporting one opinion over another on a complex subject about which we know relatively little is frequently *to affirm what we wish to believe, rather than to ascertain the truth.* As the Torah apparently says, "We do not see things as they are, but as we are".

Consider, for example, the opinions that you and I hold as non-experts on the question of man-made global warming (or on any other of the eight questions above that interests you sufficiently to have caused you to form an opinion on it). As non-experts it is impossible for us to know whether our respective beliefs are actually supported by the facts or not. Our belief is accordingly based not on fact but on faith. Neither of us can, or does, know whether significant man-made global warming is actually taking place or not, yet this does not stop us from holding an opinion on the matter. Why do we do this, rather than suspending belief, and remaining agnostic on a particular subject?

If the reason, as suggested above, is that we are generally predisposed to affirm what we wish to believe to be true – to confirm our prejudices - rather than to ascertain the truth, then it would be helpful to be aware of this tendency in ourselves, so that we can take it into account when what we choose to believe about a particular issue could eventually turn out to have dire negative consequences for us. The paradox also explains why we personally have to remain ultimately responsible for all the decisions that we make.

5.4 Conclusion

Darwin's gift has not yet been fully unpacked. While Western civilisation has understood the implications of his insights sufficiently to turn its general cultural orientation from the supernatural to the secular, it has failed notably to do so in respect of morality. Moral opinion is still widely being accepted in the West as fact, the hallmark of supernaturally-based morality, instead of being universally understood to be never more than debateable (and in due course, possibly changeable) human opinion. Given the dominant role that morality plays in shaping society socially and politically, this does not auger well for what is likely to be a turbulent future for Western civilisation, with few fixed reference points.

The dangers identified in this essay regarding the persistent public acceptance of moral opinion as fact in society, is not merely a philosophical curiosity. What such continued and unthinking acceptance means is that any individual in any society who is sufficiently charismatic and dynamic (and no matter how psychotic) is potentially in a position to convince the masses, and the intellectuals who should be guiding them, that he has access to the moral truth, and that the moral opinions that he expresses are not merely his opinion but are objective moral facts. This is a very dangerous position for society ever to be in. And, soon enough, credulous society will once again be trudging down its mystical and authoritarian Via Dolorosa. Humans, unfortunately, have a powerful inclination to attach themselves to a charismatic leader, no matter how dangerous he might be to their interests, or how irrational his doctrine. We are, it would seem, in this respect, very much herd animals.

That this situation prevails, despite Darwin and despite the greater understanding induced by four hundred years of exposure to the significance of the scientific method, is probably telling us something about ourselves. And the highly successful scientific method itself is a system of observing and reasoning that simply requires mankind to put aside its emotions for the duration.

Possibly, these things are telling us that our rationality is irreversibly circumscribed by our emotional needs, and we therefore choose to accept moral opinion as fact, not because we actually think it to be fact, but because doing so allows us to live emotionally in the comforting perception of a supposed reality shaped by delusion, rather than in the impersonal and unsentimental perception of reality provided by reason. It is difficult otherwise to explain why mankind, despite its indisputable rational faculty, has always chosen to believe the fantastical, highly unlikely, and frequently puerile explanations offered by its leaders, regarding its relationship with the rest of reality.

Ultimately, it appears to be a matter of growing up emotionally. Is the human species to remain forever childlike in respect of its moral beliefs, with the unfortunate political and social consequences that this naivety, credulity, and excessive optimism invariably has, or will we succeed in achieving emotional adulthood? Hopefully, we have a choice. By continuing to accept the possibility of mere moral opinion being fact, we can cling to our explicit or implicit belief in the supernatural. Or, alternatively, we can consciously reject superstition and select reason as our guiding basis for moral judgement.

We have achieved something akin to this before, when Western society came gradually from the 16th century onwards to accept the pragmatic conclusions that the scientific method presented us with, over the mystical and dogmatic truths offered by the religious institutions. This change involved a surprising victory of reason over emotion, which need not necessarily have taken place. Up to the present moment, however, in respect of morality we have unconsciously chosen to stay with superstition, and the continued and widespread acceptance of Socialism's continued presentation of moral opinion as fact in today's secular world is the principal evidence of this.